Payments Systems in the U.S.

A Guide for the
Payments Professional

CAROL COYE BENSON
SCOTT LOFTESNESS

The answers you need about payments systems:

What are they?

How do they work?

Who uses them?

Who provides them?

Who profits from them?

How are they changing?

GLENBROOK PAYMENTS ESSENTIALS

This book is part of Glenbrook Partners' Payments Essentials series of books, webinars, and workshops—including the popular Glenbrook Payments Boot Camp, attended by more than 4,000 payments professionals.

GLENBROOK PRESS

Printed in the United States of America.

Published by Glenbrook Partners
Menlo Park, California
www.glenbrook.com
ISBN 978-0-9827897-0-4

While every precaution has been taken in the preparation of this book, the publisher assumes no responsibility for errors or omissions, or for damages resulting from the use of the information contained in it.

Book design and production by Joel Friedlander
http://www.TheBookDesigner.com

Cover photo by Kevin Dooley, licensed under Creative Commons
http://www.flickr.com/photos/pagedooley/

About Glenbrook

Carol Coye Benson and Scott Loftesness are two of the founding partners of Glenbrook Partners. Established in 2001, Glenbrook is a consulting, research, and education firm focused on the payments industry. Glenbrook brings to financial services and financial technology clients a unique combination of specialized skills in payments, many years of senior, hands-on experience, and a network of professional relationships.

About The Authors

Carol Coye Benson's work is concentrated on mobile payments in the U.S. market, business-to-business payments, and bill payments, with a focus on product strategy around consumer and business adoption of new payments methods. Carol has more than 25 years' experience in financial services product, marketing, and strategy development with leading financial services providers. Before founding Glenbrook Partners, Carol was a managing director of the Global Institutional Services division of Deutsche Bank, where she lead marketing, client online services, and Internet development. At Visa International, she led groups working on eCommerce card security, database marketing, and technology investments. Also with Visa International, Carol founded and managed a European product development office, where she managed a series of eCommerce and chip-card projects for banks across Europe. Earlier, she spent twelve years with Citibank, where she managed the development and market introduction of new commercial payments products. Carol began her career as a corporate lending officer for large multinationals at both Bank of America and Citibank. In addition to her work as a consultant, Carol is the partner in charge of Glenbrook's Payments Education program, which provides executive training for professionals in the payments industry.

Scott Loftesness is currently focusing his work at Glenbrook on payments innovation, mobile payments, and social media/Web 2.0 in banking and financial services. With more than 30 years' experience in information technology—as a technologist, senior executive, board member, venture investor, consultant, advisor, and mentor—Scott brings seasoned judgment and a unique business perspective to his work with Glenbrook. He works extensively with payments industry start-ups and investors, helping refine business models, approaches to technical design, and go-to-market strategies. Earlier in his career, Scott was group executive vice president at First Data Merchant Services. As group executive vice president at Visa International, he led development of global payments systems strategies, including research and development initiatives related to card payments, Internet payments, and advanced card technologies. Scott began his career as a systems engineer with IBM, where, over seventeen years, he held a series of technical management and product planning positions. In addition to his consulting work, he is the partner in charge of Glenbrook's online services for payments professionals, Payments News and Payments Jobs.

Thanks

Carol and Scott want to thank Allen Weinberg, who founded Glenbrook Partners with them in 2001, and their other partners: Russ Jones, Dennis Moser, Bryan Derman, Jay DeWitt, Erin McCune, and Jacqueline Chilton. Thanks as well to our friends in the industry who devoted time to reviewing the book, including Broox Peterson, David Walker of ECCHO, Jan Estep and Mike Herd of NACHA, Lauren Hargraves of the Federal Reserve Bank of New York, and Marcy Rodriguez of TSYS. Thanks as well to the book team, including designer and coach Joel Friedlander, and to colleagues Ann Brown, Lisa Gluskin Stonestreet, and Julie Cosgrove. Most of all, thanks to our clients and all of the payments professionals who work on bringing innovation to payments and making this the exciting industry it is!

Table of Contents

List of Figures

List of Tables

1 Introduction

PAYMENTS ARE A BIG part of all of our lives. We pay for things we want and need. We scramble for change in our purse or pockets; we shuffle through the cards in our wallet to find the right one for a purchase. We write checks or pay bills online. We buy gift cards and schedule mortgage payments. We worry about funding big purchases; we try to find the right path for ordinary purchases. We're all different. For some of us, convenience is king; for others, control, or the collection of rewards, or following the patterns our parents taught us, determine how and why we make payments.

As businesspeople, we may be involved in how our businesses make payments—to employees, to suppliers, to governments. We may also be involved in how our businesses collect payments—from consumers or from businesses.

These activities are central to our personal and business lives. And for some of us, they are also the services that fuel our livelihoods. "Under the hood" of these simple payment transactions are the systems, products, and companies that form the payments industry.

This book is written for the *payments professional*. Payments professionals may work for companies that enable payments transactions. This includes banks, of course, but also many other types of companies—processors, payments services, software companies, point-of-sale terminal manufacturers, service providers, risk managers, and others. Some of these companies are powerful incumbents, while others are their competitors—start-ups that are bringing innovation to the industry. Many of these fail or stagnate, but a few succeed—and join the incumbents watching nervously for the next round of new challengers. Other payments professionals are responsible within an enterprise for the collection or disbursement of payments. Still others work as advisors, consultants, lawyers, or investors in the industry.

As in any industry, the professionals in the payments industry struggle to keep up with changes in the environment, in technology, and in the payments behavior of consumers, merchants, and other users of payments systems. Some payments professionals are well-versed in one payments system (cards, perhaps, or ACH); others in a function such as consumer marketing or risk management. This book provides a comprehensive view of the entire payments industry, including all its systems and functions.

This book is not a source for statistics or "league tables" on payments. There are many such industry sources; each chapter includes a list of resources that offer more information about a particular payments system or topic. We have tried to be as unbiased as possible; any opinions, speculations, or anecdotes on a topic are set in shaded boxes.

We very much welcome your questions and comments. Email **books@glenbrook.com** and we'll respond!

Payments Systems Overview

Payments transfer value from one end party to another. A payments system, as shown in Figure 2-1, defines how such value transfers are done and provides a framework of rules for users of the system.

A payment system may be centralized, decentralized, or "virtual." A payment system connects large numbers of end parties, formalizes processes for transfer of value, and plays some role in managing risks for the participants.

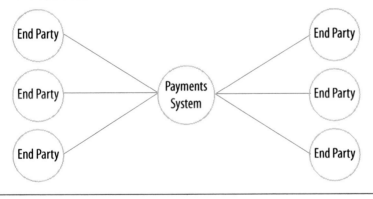

Figure 2-1.
What Is A Payment
System?

There are many types of payments systems. Most share these common characteristics:

- They operate within a single country, but on a national basis within that country.

- They are denominated in the currency of that country.

- They are subject, directly or indirectly, to regulation by the government of that country.

- They enable multiple parties to transact with each other.

Payments Systems in the United States

There are six core payments systems in the United States:

- Cash

- The checking system

- The credit card and charge card systems

- The debit card systems

- The ACH (Automated Clearing House) system

- The wire transfer systems

As we will see in Chapter 10, there are many additional ways of making payments, including methods such as online banking/bill payment and products such as email and mobile telephone payments services. Almost all of these methods rely on one or more of the core payments systems to actually transfer value between parties.

The Domains of Payment

Payments are used, of course, for multiple purposes. We categorize these uses into six domains of payment, each of which exhibits unique characteristics and requirements:

- **POS.** Payments made at the physical point of sale. Includes store and restaurant payments, but also unattended environments such as vending machines and transit kiosks.

- **eCommerce.** Payments made online for purchases of goods and services. Includes eRetailing but also online travel, online subscriptions, and the purchase of digital content.

- **Bill payments.** Payments made by individuals or businesses based on receipt of what is typically a monthly bill.

- **P2P payments.** Person-to-person payments. Includes domestic payments among friends and families, but also cross-border remittances (e.g., migrant worker payments to relatives in home countries), and account-to-account transfers by individuals (referred to as "A2A" or, sometimes, "me to me" payments).

- **B2B payments.** Business-to-business payments. Includes payments from buyer to supplier, but also intracompany payments and, significantly, financial market payments (bank-to-bank payments, securities purchases, foreign exchange transactions, etc.). For the purposes of this

> **Terminology** Throughout this book, we use the term "end party" to refer to both the receiver and the sender of funds. An end party may be a consumer, or may be a merchant or other enterprise—for example, a biller, small business, government, or nonprofit. In any payment transaction, one end party is the payer, and one the receiver, of funds; as we will see, either the payer or the receiver may initiate the payment, depending on payments system and type.
>
> We will use the term "provider" to refer to parties who are providing access to the payments systems to end users and/or other providers. Banks, networks, clearing houses, processors and service providers are all types of providers. Finally, we use the term "bank," unless otherwise noted, to refer to all depository financial institutions in the United States, including credit unions, thrifts, and savings banks.

framework, governments, nonprofits, and other types of enterprises are included as "businesses."

- **Income payments.** Payments to individuals for salary, benefits, and expense reimbursements.

The payments systems support activity across these payments domains, and, in fact, compete with each other at a systems level. A good example of this occurs in the B2B payments domain where checking, the traditional payments system used, is in decline. All of the electronic payments systems are competing for volumes shifting away from check. The ACH system has specialized transaction codes for B2B payments, and carries remittance data along with the payments. The card networks have business purchasing cards and small-business credit and debit card products. The wire transfer systems are enhancing their networks to carry remittance data to meet the requirements of this domain. Meanwhile, the checking system itself, through imaging, remote deposit capture, and other advances, is competing to maintain volume.

Payments System Volumes

Payments system volumes are measured in two ways: by **count** and **amount.** "Count" refers to the number of transactions made, and "amount" to the Total dollar value of those transactions. In the card systems in particular, the term "volume" refers to the amount, or the dollar value of the transactions.

Some systems do a better job of measuring themselves than others. The card and wire transfer systems, for example, have quite precise measures. But checking, and especially cash, have no formal mechanisms for national measurement, and are therefore simply estimated.

Estimated Volumes by Payments Systems as a Percent of Total - 2009		
System	Count	Amount
Cash	31.5%	0.2%
ACH	11.8%	3.5%
Check	16.7%	2.6%
Credit	14.9%	0.2%
Debit	25.0%	0.1%
Wire	0.1%	93.4%
Totals in Billions	154.13	$1,065,666.8

Table 2-1.
Payments Systems
Volumes
Source: Glenbrook. Cash
figures are for consumer use
only

Table 2-1 shows Glenbrook's estimates for U.S. payments systems volumes as a percent of total payments systems transactions for the year 2009. Note the dominance of wire transfer transactions in the total amount column—those payments represent less than 1% of the total count, but more than 93% of the total amount. The totals shown are large—much larger than GNP, for instance. This is because a single economic transaction (such as a consumer purchase) can result in multiple payments system transactions, as the various parties in the value chain move funds to effect payment, settlement, etc.

Payments System Models

Payments systems can operate on a variety of models.

Open Loop Systems

Open loop systems operate on a hub-and-spoke model. Almost all large-scale payments systems use this model. An open loop system requires intermediaries (almost always banks or depository financial institutions) to join the payments system. These intermediaries then form business relationships with end parties (consumers, for example, or merchants).

An open loop payments system relies on intermediaries, usually banks, to connect end parties.

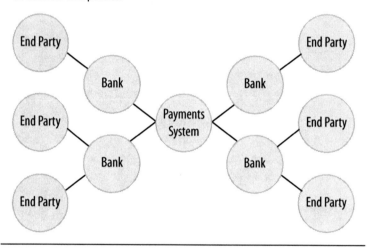

Figure 2-2.
Open Loop Systems

A transaction is passed from one end party to his or her bank, on to the network, on to the other end party's bank, and on to that end party. This structure allows the two end parties to transact with each other without having direct relationships with each other's banks. The banks, similarly, can transact with each other without a direct relationship.

Today, most electronic payments systems—both paper-based and electronic (cards, ACH, wire transfers and even check images)—operate on this model. This is true despite the fact that current technology would quite easily

> **Origins: Check Clearing Houses** Initially formed in the 1800s, check clearing houses were the first large-scale open loop systems in the United States. Before clearing houses existed, each bank receiving a deposit containing a check drawn on other banks needed to present that check directly to the check writer's bank in order to collect payment on it. As the volume of checks in use rose, this required a complex web of bilateral relationships among banks in a city. Clearing a check drawn on a bank in another city was even more complicated, and often required one or more correspondent banks to effect payment. The earliest check clearing house was a simple meeting, each business morning, of representatives from each participating bank in a city. Clerks from each of the banks would come to the clearing house bearing bags of checks. At the clearing house, the checks would be exchanged and each clerk would depart with the checks written on accounts at his bank. (It is interesting to note that in the early phases of the card industry, paper "sales drafts" were cleared in much the same way.)

permit the exchange of electronic transactions on a bilateral basis. But, as we will see, the open loop model also creates an effective means of allocating liability.

The advantage of the open loop structure is that it allows a payments system to scale quite rapidly. As intermediaries join the payments system, all of their end party customers are immediately accessible to other intermediaries participating in the payments system.

Closed Loop Systems

A closed loop payments system operates without intermediaries. The end parties, most typically consumers and merchants, instead directly join the payments system. The original American Express and Discover systems, and the proprietary card systems (for example, a Sears credit card accepted only at Sears) are examples of closed loop systems. Most payments services providers operate as closed loop systems, although some may access open loop systems for transaction funding or delivery.

Closed loop systems have the advantage of simplicity. As one entity sets all of the rules, it can act more quickly and more flexibly than the distributed open loop systems, which must propagate change throughout the system's intermediary layers. The disadvantage of closed loop systems is that they are more difficult to grow than open loop systems; each end party must be individually signed up by the payments system.

As we will see in Chapter 5, some of the closed loop card payments systems are in the process of evolving toward more open loop models.

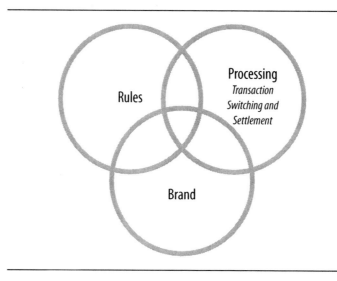

Figure 2-3.
Payment Systems
Functions

Payments systems must provide three key functions, shown in Figure 2-3: processing, rules, and brand. Some payments systems provide all three functions through a single organization. Others accommodate these functions via a virtual, or distributed, model.

- **Processing includes switching—the means by which a transaction moves from one party to another.** In a closed loop system, this transfers value between the end parties. In an open loop system, this transfers value between intermediaries on behalf of their end parties. As the term is used here, processing also includes settlement—the process by which intermediaries in an open loop system transfer value—usually on a net basis—to cover the individual transactions each has been party to.

- **Rules (sometimes called "operating rules") bind each of the participants in a system.** In an open loop system, the rules bind the intermediaries. Although the rules may require intermediaries to require certain things of their end parties, the end parties are not directly bound by the rules. In a closed loop system, the rules bind the end parties directly.

- **Brand is the means by which the parties to a transaction communicate to each other how they will pay.** This is sometimes "branding with a capital B" (e.g., "do you take MasterCard?") and sometimes with a "small b" ("I'll give you a check.") For the card networks in particular, significant brand advertising has been a critical driver of payments system growth.

Other Terms in Open Loop Payments Systems

On-us transactions occur when the bank intermediary is the same on both sides of a transaction. Depending on the payments system, the transaction may stay within the bank (e.g., never be submitted to a clearing house or "hub" for switching), in which case the bank settles the transaction through an internal book transfer. In other systems, an on-us transaction is passed through the system and returns to the bank, just like a regular "off-us" transaction. The growing concentration of U.S. banks is increasing the percentage of "on-us" transactions.

Correspondent banking relationships between banks allow smaller banks, which may not participate directly in a payments system, to access that system on behalf of their customers through a relationship with a participant bank. Many smaller banks in the United States gain access to the wire transfer systems in this way. This model is also used extensively for cross-border payments.

Payments Systems Flow

The switching function in an open loop payments system is a message flow from the first intermediary to the network (which could be, in a centralized model, the payments system itself, or, in a distributed model, a hub or a clearing house) to the second intermediary. This message always flows in the same direction. What the message says, however, is different depending on whether the payment is a "**push**" or a "**pull**" payment.

While the concept of push and pull payments can be confusing, it is essential to understanding the workings of payments systems—in particular the risks and liabilities borne by the parties to a transaction. "Push" or "pull" refers to the action of the intermediary entering the transaction into the system. Push and pull payments are illustrated in Figure 2-4.

The payment message flows the same way in both **push** and **pull** payments. In this diagram, End Party A is the party that enters a transaction into the payment system—for example, a merchant depositing a check or an employer sending a direct payroll deposit to its bank.

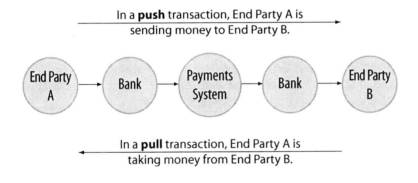

In a **push** transaction, End Party A is sending money to End Party B.

In a **pull** transaction, End Party A is taking money from End Party B.

Figure 2-4. Push and Pull Transactions

- **Any time that "End Party A" is sending money to "End Party B," it is considered a push payment—for example, a wire transfer or an ACH direct deposit of payroll.** Taking the direct deposit as an example, we see that the employer ("End Party A") is instructing its bank to send money to employees through the ACH network. In effect, the first bank is saying to the second bank, "I am debiting myself; you should credit yourself."

- **When "End Party A" collects money from "End Party B," it is considered a pull payment.** Checks, cards, and ACH debit transactions are pull payments. Using a check as an example, we see that the merchant ("End Party A") is, by depositing the check, instructing its bank to send that check through a clearing method to collect payment from "End Party B" (the check writer). In effect, the first bank is saying to the second bank, "I am crediting myself; you should debit yourself."

Payments and Risk

Push payments are fundamentally much less risky than pull payments. In a push payment, the party who has funds is sending the money, so there is essentially no risk of NSF, or nonsufficient funds—push payments can't "bounce." Furthermore, in a push payments system the transaction is initiated by the sender's bank, which knows that its end party has the money. Other types of fraud, of course, are still possible.

Pull payments are inherently subject to "bouncing." The bank initiating the transaction does not know whether or not the bank receiving the transaction will be able to successfully apply that transaction to the credit or debit account of its customer. Furthermore, pull transactions depend on the payer ("End Party B" in Figure 2-4) having authorized the "sender" of the message to effect the transaction. (A signed check presented to a merchant, or a card swipe with signature or PIN, are examples of such an authorization.)

Card networks are pull payment networks. Card payments don't bounce—but this doesn't mean that they are push transactions. They are instead guaranteed pull transactions. The card networks accomplished this by adding a separate message flow, called the authorization, that runs through the network before the pull payment transaction is submitted. This authorization transaction asks, "Are there sufficient funds, or available credit balances, to pay this transaction?" If so, the pull transaction is submitted. Card network rules specify that merchants receiving this "yes" reply are covered for both insufficient funds and fraud risks. (Important differences in eCommerce and other environments in which the card is not present will be discussed in Chapters 5 and 8.)

Payments System Settlement

Settlement in an open loop system occurs when the system operator (or a designated settlement service) calculates the daily net amount due to or due from each bank. The banks are then instructed to fund or draw from an account at the system's settlement bank.

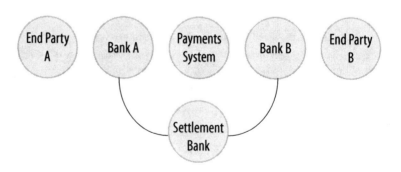

Figure 2-5.
Payments System
Settlement

Settlement in an open loop system refers to the process by which the *intermediaries* actually receive or send funds to each other. The settlement function in an open loop system can be done on either a **net** or a **gross** settlement basis:

- **In a net settlement system, the net obligations of participating intermediaries are calculated on a periodic basis—most typically daily.** At the end of the day, a participating intermediary is given a net settlement total and instructed either (a) to fund a settlement account with that amount, should it be in a net debit position, or (b) that there are funds available to draw on in its settlement account, should it be in a net credit position. Checking, card payments systems, and the ACH are all net settlement systems in the United States. In a variant on the net settlement approach, settlement of checks and ACH, when handled through a Federal Reserve bank, is done on a batch basis: a bank's account at a Federal Reserve Bank is periodically credited or debited with total amounts from a batch of transactions which have been processed.

- **In a gross settlement system, each transaction settles as it is processed.** With the Fedwire system, for example, a transaction is effected when the sending bank's account at a Federal Reserve Bank is debited and the receiving bank's account at a Federal Reserve Bank system is credited. No end-of-day settlement process is necessary.

How end party settlement is effected depends on the payments system. The timing and manner of a credit or debit to a consumer, merchant, or enterprise account may be defined by the payments system, by regulation, or simply by market practices.

In a closed loop system, the only settlement is the end party settlement. The operator of the system defines how such a settlement is handled.

The Virtual Systems

Two core United States payments systems, cash and checking, operate on a virtual basis. By this we mean that there is no formal payments system that end parties, or bank intermediaries, "join."

We all know, of course, how cash works. The transaction is "switched" and "settled" directly between the two end parties. From that perspective, it is a push system. Other aspects of cash payments are covered in Chapter 6.

The checking system in the United States automatically includes all depository financial institutions—they do not have to "join." Banks do, however, usually join one or more clearing houses to switch and settle the checks they receive in deposits. The clearing houses have rules, but these are much more limited in scope than the rules of the card or ACH networks. In part, this is because paper checks are covered more extensively by U.S. law and regulation. Other aspects of checking are covered in Chapter 3.

These virtual systems have no "capital B" brand, and no central network that promotes their use.

Payments System Ownership and Regulation

Ownership

Most United States payments systems began as bank-owned systems. Over the past decade, as Table 2-2 shows, many of these systems have migrated to different ownership models. Some of the non-bank-owned payments systems are publicly traded companies; others are privately held.

Payments System	Original Owner	Current Owner
ACH*	Bank	Bank
American Express	Non-Bank	Non-Bank
MasterCard	Bank	Non-Bank
Visa	Bank	Non-Bank
Discover	Non-Bank	Non-Bank
STAR	Bank	Non-Bank
NYCE	Bank	Non-Bank
FedWire	Bank (Fed)	Bank (Fed)
CHIPs	Bank	Bank
Cash	None	None
Checking**	None	None

*The ACH operators are also indirectly bank-owned
** Some check clearing houses are bank-owned; some are owned by private sector processors

Table 2-2. Payments System Ownership

Payments systems that are owned by large groups of banks tend to make rules that benefit the banks as a group. This can have the effect of "leveling the playing field"—all participating banks have equal access to products and services. Systems with large budgets for staff and advertising (notably the card networks) create fully defined products that the member banks then distribute to their customers. Systems with smaller budgets (such as the ACH) do much less in the way of product definition and management, and only provide the operating rules and/or platforms that the banks then use to create products.

Regulation

Payments systems in the United States are regulated by a mix of governmental and private rules. Government rule, of course, is by law, and by regulations issued by agencies of the government to implement those laws. In the United States, the primary issuer of payments regulations is the Federal

Reserve Board. Private rules can either take the form of network rules, or of simple contracts applying to a service used: the Federal Reserve Bank's operating circulars (governing the use of the Federal Reserve Bank payments services offered to banks) are an example of this. Private rules can be thought of as "agreement-based".

Private System Rules

Most payments systems require either intermediaries (open loop systems) or end parties (closed loop systems) to formally join the system. The party joining the system is bound by the rules of the system. In an open loop system, the intermediary's contract with its end party often contains provisions dictated by the operating rules, making the end parties indirectly governed by some of the rules. These operating rules are extremely important, particularly for open loop networks, as they define the parameters necessary for successful interoperability among thousands or millions of end parties.

Operating rules cover a wide range of topics, including:

- **Technical standards.** Data formats, token (e.g., card) specifications, delivery and receipt capabilities, data security standards, etc.

- **Processing standards.** Time limits for submitting and returning transactions, requirements for posting to end party accounts, etc.

- **Membership requirements.** Types of institutions that can join, capital requirements, etc.

- **Payment acceptance requirements.** Constraints on the ability to selectively accept payments transactions.

- **Exception processing and dispute resolution.** Rights and requirements of intermediaries and end parties, often with respect to disputing or refusing a transaction.

- **Fees.** Processing and other charges paid to the payments system; interchange, if any, among the intermediaries.

- **Brands and marks.** Standards for use of the payments system brand.

A new product at the payments system level (for example, contactless cards) or a new transaction type (for example, NACHA's WEB transaction) generally requires a new set of operating rules that apply to that particular product or transaction type. Operating rules requirements can have significant financial impact on both users of and providers to a payments system. Investment may be required to meet technical standards, or to provide certain forms of services, such as dispute resolution; changes in definition of liability or allocation of risk can also have large effects.

Some open loop payments systems, Visa, MasterCard, and NACHA, make most of their operating rules publicly available on their websites. (Note that in the global open loop card networks, each region has its own operating rules; an additional set of international operating rules covers cross-border transactions.) Other payments systems, such as CHIPs and most of the PIN debit networks, do not make their operating rules available to nonmembers.

Changes to the operating rules of a payments system can be difficult and take years to implement. Most payments systems have several tiers of committees through which participants consider proposed rules changes. There is often a year or more of lag time between approval and implementation of a new rule.

The check payments system in the U.S., as discussed above, is a "virtual" system with no central authority. Banks do, however, join one or more check clearing houses to process checks. These clearing houses act like payments systems in that their operating rules bind the members. Such rules tend to be narrow in scope, however, compared to those in the card, ACH, and wire transfer systems. Check clearing house rules may specify times for presenting or returning items, image standards, etc.

> Today, banks, processors and clearing houses are dealing with a complex regulatory framework following the dramatic shift to image clearing. For example, some regulations that apply to paper check clearing no longer apply to image clearing. This is a transitional period for the industry as it evaluates the right regulatory model for an all-image clearing world.

United States Law and Federal Reserve Bank Regulation

- U.S. law regulates some payments systems specifically, and others more generally. Federal Reserve Bank regulations implement law and specify requirements that are binding on the banks that they regulate. Key laws and regulations include:

  - U.C.C. Article 3—Negotiable Instruments.

- U.C.C. Article 4—Bank Deposits and Collections.

- U.C.C. Article 4A—Funds Transfers.

- The Check Clearing for the 21st Century Act (Check 21).

- The Credit Card Accountability Responsibility and Disclosure Act of 2009.

- Federal Reserve Bank Regulation E (implementing provisions in the Electronic Fund Transfer Act) applies to consumer electronic transactions including debit cards, ATM withdrawals, and ACH transactions (but not credit cards). Among other provisions, Regulation E establishes key consumer rights for repudiation and reversal of non-authorized transactions.

- Regulation CC—Availability of Funds and Collection of Checks.

- Federal Reserve Bank Regulation Z, Truth in Lending, prescribes uniform methods for computing the cost of credit, for disclosing credit terms, and for resolving errors on certain types of credit accounts.

- Federal Reserve Bank Regulation J, Collection of Checks and Other Items by Federal Reserve Banks and Funds Transfers through Fedwire, establishes procedures, duties, and responsibilities among (1) Federal Reserve Banks, (2) the senders and payers of checks and other items, and (3) the senders and recipients of Fedwire funds transfers.

A number of other significant laws, regulations, and orders fall under the general category of bank regulation. These include regulation around money laundering, privacy, credit reporting, and other issues relevant to payments.

Regulatory requirements around "Know Your Customer" (KYC) are particularly important for banks and non-banks in the payments industry. Provisions mandated by the Bank Secrecy Act and USA PATRIOT require a variety of identity checking procedures prior to opening a customer account.

State Banking Authorities

State law and regulations by state banking authorities apply mostly to non-bank providers of payments services, and are referred to as "money transmitter regulations." They regulate sales and issuance of payments instruments, as well as transmitting or receiving money. Many states require that money transmitters obtain a state license, post a bond, and/or maintain certain levels of net worth or permissible investments. Notably, state money transmission regulation is not uniform, creating additional challenges for payments companies with national ambitions. State banking authorities also regulate state-chartered banks.

> **The Future of Payments Regulation**
>
> It is interesting to reflect on what the future may hold for U.S. payments regulation. One can argue that the U.S. permits much more self-regulation of key payments systems than do other countries. This may be because banks in the U.S. are heavily regulated, by multiple authorities. The payments systems, historically owned by banks, were therefore de facto under a regulatory "umbrella." Today many payments systems are no longer bank-owned. Does this mean that federal regulators may begin to take a more active role in the industry?

Economic Models for Payments Systems

Payments systems providers, including banks, networks, and processors, make money by providing access to payments systems for end parties. End parties include consumers, merchants, and enterprises (billers, other businesses, governments, and nonprofit groups). Processors and networks also make money by providing payments services to intermediaries such as banks. Many banks provide payments services to other banks as a part of correspondent banking relationships. Merchants may also provide payments services—for example, when they provide private-label or gift cards to consumers.

Each bank sets its own price for services to its end party. Bank revenue can include fees and interest, as well as indirect components such as float.

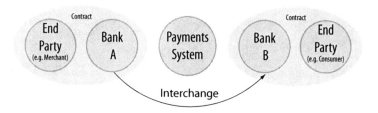

In some systems, the network also defines a fee that flows from one bank to the other. This is called **interchange**.

Figure 2-6.
Economics of
Open Loop Systems

In this book, we will examine the economics of each core payments system in turn. But a few general observations can be made about payments system economics:

• In both open loop and closed loop payments systems, providers have a direct business relationship with end party customers. Providers set prices for their services, as do other businesses. Providers realize revenue from payments through direct and indirect sources. This is true whether the end party is a consumer or an enterprise. Direct revenue comes from fees explicitly charged to the end party; these may include transaction fees, interest on associated loans, monthly maintenance fees, and exception fees (overdraft fees, bounced check fees, late payment fees). Indirect revenue comes from net interest income on deposit balances, float, and interchange.

• In some open loop payments systems, the rule-making body may define interchange for the system: a fee paid by one intermediary to the other in partial compensation for handling the transaction.

• Providers often price payments products as part of an overall bundle of services—for example, a checking account with bundled ATM access, checkwriting privileges, and a debit card. Similarly, a processor may price card acceptance

What is Interchange? Interchange is an element of payments system economics used by some open loop systems, particularly by card networks. Interchange is a transfer of value from one intermediary in a payments transaction to the other intermediary in that transaction. The payments system sets the interchange prices, but does not itself receive the value of interchange. Interchange creates an incentive for one "side" of the transaction to participate, by having the other "side" reimburse some of the costs incurred.

Payments Systems and Interchange: Some Have It, Some Don't In the U.S., the wire transfer, ACH, and checking open loop systems operate without interchange—that is, there is no network-defined transfer of value between the "sending" and "receiving" banks to such transactions. Card network transactions do bear interchange. The sometimes dramatic difference in economics that results is fueling a number of different alternative payment schemes.

Interchange is discussed in more detail in Chapter 5, Cards.

services to a small merchant on a bundled price model—but may price the same service to a large merchant on an unbundled basis.

- Costs associated with providing payments services are a mix of fixed and variable costs. Typically, payments system providers have very high fixed costs and very low incremental costs for each transaction. A bank, for example, needs to cover the costs of staffing and maintaining a branch, engaging the service that replenishes its ATMs, and working with a check processing center. While unit costs may be calculated (add up the expenses and divide by the number of transactions), they are not always accurate indicators of incremental costs. Many banks realized this as a problem in the last decade when check volumes began to drop sharply, creating a "death spiral" in which the same fixed-cost base was spread over a smaller and smaller number of checks. With the advent of image clearing, however, banks were able to stop this process and reduce check processing costs.

> **Risk Pays** Whenever a provider—for example, a credit card issuer or a payments services provider—proactively assumes risk that another party would otherwise bear, it is apt to be well compensated. A provider that assumes risk but does not manage it well, or (worst case!) does not understand that it is assuming risk, is apt to have a short business life.
>
> **What is Float? (Part 1 of 2)** Float is the value earned from money held over a period of time. It is a benefit to a party that holds funds for a period of time before needing to pay them out. It is a cost to a party that needs to pay out funds prior to receiving them.

- The payments industry is different from other processing industries in one very important aspect—the value of the money being transferred through the system. Providers who realize revenue related to the gross value of the payment transaction (the "amount") are more likely to have profitable businesses than those who realize revenue simply on a fee-per-transaction basis (a "click fee"). This type of *ad valorem* (percent of value) revenue may be direct (a fee calculated as a percentage of the amount of the transaction, or an interest rate applied to a loan balance) or indirect (the value of deposit balances held at a bank, or float).

- The economics of exception processing are critically important to the payments industry. An exception item may occur simply because of a processing error (for example, a check shredded in a sorter). It may, in the case of a pull transaction, bounce. Or it may be the result of a customer inquiry or dispute. Typically, the cost of handling these exception items is much higher than the cost of handling a standard transaction. The efficiency with which a provider manages the exception process may significantly define the overall economics of the product for that provider. In recent years, providers have been increasingly aggressive in pricing exception transactions to end parties. In some cases, the revenue from an exception transaction far exceeds the cost of the transaction, and contributes significantly to the profitability of the product. This is the case, for example, with bounced check fees, card overlimit fees, and, in most cases, overdraft fees.

Risk Management

All payments transactions are subject to risk. Some risks, notably that of fraud, have a very high public profile. But there are many types of risk, and all parties to a payments transaction bear some portion of the risk.

Open Loop Systems and the Chain of Liability

In open loop systems, intermediaries and the network assume certain liabilities for the actions of their customers, as well as for their own actions. The nature of these liabilities is determined by the operating rules of the payments system. In the ACH system, for example, the originating bank of an ACH debit transaction warrants that its customer has properly obtained the consumer's consent for the debit to his or her account. If the consumer successfully disputes a transaction, the originating bank must reimburse the consumer's bank. The originating bank will, of course, try to recoup this from its customer—but if unsuccessful, the bank is left "holding the bag." Similarly, in the card networks, if a customer initiates a dispute that (according to the rules) requires a transaction to be reversed, the acquiring bank is ultimately responsible to the network for the obligation of its merchant customer.

Credit risk. A credit card issuer bears obvious credit risk: the cardholder may simply fail to repay his or her loan balance. But there are other types of credit risk inherent in payments. Whenever a bank, for example, extends an overdraft rather than bouncing a pull payment (be it a debit card, check, or ACH debit), it incurs credit risk. Less obviously, a bank on the "send" side of a pull transaction (a card acquiring bank, or a check deposit bank) incurs credit risk because it is assuming financial responsibility for the actions of its customer.

- **Fraud risk.** As shown in the consumer and merchant example in Table 2-3 there are many types of payments fraud risk, some specific to certain payments systems and others more general. Some payments systems, such as the card systems, have very high levels of system-defined fraud management. Others, such as checking and ACH, leave more of the fraud risk management to intermediaries and end parties.

Fraudster Evolution: A Game of Whack-A-Mole

Fraudsters are endlessly inventive and quick to capitalize on new technologies or practices by merchants, banks, or consumers. Payments systems fraud management is characterized by cycles of spiking fraud, followed by the introduction of new fraud countermeasures, followed by a migration of fraudsters to other payments systems or environments.

System	Consumer	Consumer's Bank	Network	Merchant's Bank	Merchant
Cash	Theft	Theft	Settlement Risk	Theft	Theft
Checking	Fraud	Fraud		Fraud, NSF	Fraud, NSF
Credit Card	Fraud	Fraud, Credit		Fraud	
Debit Card	Fraud	Fraud		Fraud	
ACH (Push)		Fraud			
ACH (Pull)	Fraud	Fraud		Fraud, NSF	Fraud, NSF
Wires		Fraud			

Notes on card fraud: receiver's exposure is different in a card-not-present environment. Consumers have some protections against fraud. Merchant's bank is exposed to merchant fraud.

Table 2-3.
Payments Systems
Fraud Exposures

- **Operations risk.** Occurs when one party to a transaction either fails to do what is expected or does something in error. A wide range of situations fall into this category: missed deadlines, incorrectly formatted files, machines that fail to start or operate correctly (e.g., check sorters jamming), etc. An operational error can have extremely serious financial consequences if, as a result, a party to the transaction ends up holding funds that it is obligated (by rules) to pass on to another party. Each payments system has a combination of rules and working practices by which intermediaries in the system try to help each other recover from errors and avoid financial losses—but full recompense is not always possible.

The role of processors and other third parties (meaning non-bank intermediaries in the value chain) is important to understanding operations risk. Often, a third party will provide "on behalf of" processing for a bank that bears formal legal responsibility, under the payments system rules, for a given task. If the third party errs in some way, the bank still remains liable. Because of this, many payments systems recognize the role of third parties and create rules—binding their direct members (the banks) to regulate and at times certify third-party involvement in the payments system.

- **Liquidity risk.** The risk that a party cannot fulfill its financial obligations to another party. In an open loop system, end parties have financial liability to their banks, and the banks have financial liability to the network. The network in turn has financial liability to the banks. The network's exposure is referred to as **settlement risk**. This stand-in function is the key to an open loop system: it means that a bank receiving money from another bank in the system need not worry about the liquidity of

> **Balancing the Fraud Equation**
>
> The cost of fraud is constantly measured against the cost of preventing or reversing fraud. In much of the payments industry, certain levels of fraud are (more or less) accepted as the "cost of doing business." This explains, for example, a card issuer's willingness to have low-value transactions effected without signature, or a bank's decision to "take a customer's word for it" for a one-time fraudulently claimed ATM withdrawal. But when the numbers get big, the industry kicks into gear and starts developing and applying new fraud-control mechanisms.

the sending bank. The network, however, does have to worry. If a network member fails (goes out of business) during the day while in a net debit position, the network (in most cases) must pay the obligation of that member to the other members. This is one reason why most open loop networks restrict membership to regulated financial institutions that meet certain capital standards and are subject to ongoing regulatory oversight.

- **Data security risk.** The risk that end party data held by a bank, processor, network, or other end party is exposed to actual or possible fraudulent use of the data. The actions taken by the card networks to create and enforce PCI-DSS (Payment Card Industry Data Security Standards) are an attempt to proactively manage this issue.

- **Reputation risk.** The risk that end parties lose faith in the integrity of the payments system. Recently in the United States, the highly publicized loss of payment card data at merchants and processors has damaged the reputation of those companies.

- **Legal risk.** Particularly in a time of change in payments practices, intermediaries, networks, and processors may be exposed to an indeterminate amount of risk due to unclear interpretation or application of private rules or government regulation.

Comparing Payments Systems

Table 2-4 lists the factors taken into account when evaluating or comparing payments systems. As previously mentioned, the payments systems themselves compete with each other, particularly when there is a secular shift in payments behavior such as a move from cash to noncash instruments. Payments systems providers look at this issue when considering whether to support new forms of payments. Payments systems users consider it when evaluating new payments forms.

The Big Questions	
Open or closed loop?	Is a brand used (and how)?
Push or pull payments?	Does the network define "products"?
Net or gross settlement?	Do payment network rules determine:
Electronic or paper processing?	If payment is guaranteed or not?
Ownership—private vs. public; bank owned or not?	Timing of funding—before, at the time of, or after the transaction?
Regulation—private rules and/or law?	How exceptions are handled?
Batch or real-time processing?	Fraud management procedures?
Economic model—is there interchange?	How "on-us" transactions are handled?

*Table 2-4.
Comparing
Payments Systems*

Cross-Border Payments

Cross-border payments occur when a party in one country pays a party in another country. Let's look at how cross-border payments are made using open loop payments systems.

As background, remember that payments systems, by definition, operate on an in-country basis: only banks that are chartered or licensed to operate in a country may join a payments system in that country. Because of this, transferring money between countries often requires two separate transactions, one in the sending country and one in the receiving country. This is true even if the transaction is denominated in the same currency in both systems.

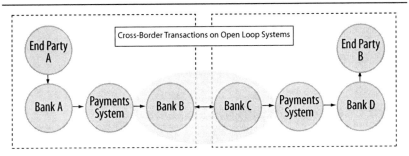

Each transaction must go through two payments systems, in two different countries. The intermediary banks (Banks B and C) settle their positions through correspondent accounts with each other, or with a third bank.

Figure 2-7.
Cross-Border
Payments

Of course, the two transactions must still be settled among the banks. This is done through a complex web of correspondent banking accounts that banks have with each other. These accounts may be housed in the sending country, the receiving country, or a third country. The global financial services messaging service SWIFT plays an important role in carrying instructions about these payments from one bank to another.

Effecting a single economic transaction in two separate payments systems (or more, in some cases) creates complexity and often confusion for the end parties. The systems may have different schedules, rules, and data formats. It is often difficult for the end party in one country (or even the bank in that country) to understand how a transaction will be treated in the receiving country. Hefty fees are not uncommon. The management of foreign exchange creates an additional level of complexity, and is often a source of considerable revenue to one or more parties to the transaction. The correspondent banking divisions of large banks manage such payments for their smaller bank customers.

Other Countries' Payments Systems

If you are interested in understanding another country's payments systems, a great place to start is at the website of the central bank of that country. Directly or indirectly, the central bank will have some regulatory control or oversight of the payments systems in its country.

Country	Checks Per Inhabitant Per Year
Belgium	1.0
Canada	38.8
France	57.4
Germany	1.0
Italy	7.2
Japan	1.0
Singapore	18.7
Sweden	0.1
Switzerland	0.2
United Kingdom	26.2
United States	93.5

Table 2-5. Variations Among Countries in Check Usage
Source: BIS

This book is focused on United States payments systems. However, the principles discussed in this book apply, generally speaking, to other countries as well.

Changing Payments Networks

Large-scale, open loop payments systems are highly efficient and scalable—the envy of many other industries that would like to achieve similar levels of smooth interoperability. (Think about the exchange of electronic medical records, for example!)

The downside of this structure is the inherent inertia in its systems. The fact that multiple remote parties can interact with each other easily, relying on a common body of standard, rules and liability frameworks, also means that it is very difficult to change these standards. Improvements or enhancements from one participant may have significant operational, technical, or economic ramifications that may not be immediately apparent at the time the change is proposed. Many proposed changes require simultaneous adjustments to technical standards, operations procedures, risk management procedures, pricing, and even the physical formatting of payments devices (checks, cards, terminals, etc.). Changing open loop payments systems can take years of work, first at a committee level (e.g., with representatives from the risk management groups at participating banks) and then at a board level. Even once approved, a payments system change may not take effect for a year or more—giving participants time to prepare.

Summary: U.S. Payments Systems

The various U.S. payments systems all move money, and they share many similar attributes. There are important differences among them, however. Understanding these differences is the key to appreciating the different utilities and economics of the systems. Table 26 gives a comparative overview of the core systems.

Payments System	Ownership & Regulation	Operations	Type	Inter-change?	Risk Management
Cash	Virtual ownership; FRB and U.S. law regulation	No transaction processing; no settlement	Push	No	Cash recipient bears counterfeit risk
Check	Virtual ownership; FRB and U.S. law regulation; private rules and agreements, especially for image exchange.	Batch processing, intrabank processing moving from paper to electronics; net settlement	Pull	No	Depositing customer bears fraud and NSF risk
ACH	Owned by banks; NACHA and FRB regulation	Batch processing, electronic; net settlement	Push and Pull	No	Originator bears fraud and NSF risk (pull transactions)
Credit Card	Public or private ownership, non-bank; network rules and FRB regulation	Real-time authorization, batch clearing, net settlement	Pull	Yes	Merchant is guaranteed good funds and is protected from fraud (card-present transactions)
Debit Card	Public or private ownership, non-bank (except for some local/regional networks); network rules and FRB regulation	Real-time authorization, batch clearing, net settlement	Pull	Yes	Merchant is guaranteed good funds and is protected from fraud (card-present transactions)
Wire Transfer	Bank ownership; FRB regulation	Real-time clearing and settlement	Push	No	Recipient of funds is guaranteed good funds and protected from fraud

Table 2-6. Summary—Core U.S. Payments Systems

There are many sources for information on the U.S. payments systems. Sources shown below are some good places to start. Further information is given at the end of the chapters on each of the core payments systems.

Sources of Information on Payments Systems

- *Payments News**
- The Clearing House
- Federal Reserve Bank Payments Services
- The American Banker (SourceMedia)
- The Nilson Report
- Bank for International Settlement
- Country Central Banks

*Glenbrook keeps a list of other payments blogs on the Payments News site.

Core Systems: Checking

Overview—Checking	
Type	Pull payments
Ownership	No owners; check clearing houses owned by banks or private processors
Regulation	Clearing house rules and Federal Reserve Bank regulation
Network Economics	Clears at par
Processing	Intrabank clearing by image or paper
Risk Management	Managed by intermediaries and end parties

Table 3-1.
Checking Overview

History and Background

The checking system in the United States is our oldest, and one of our most widely used open loop payments systems. The origins of the checking system as we know it today can be traced to medieval, and perhaps earlier, times—many economies developed some version of a document that allowed the transfer of funds from one bank to another. The word itself comes from the Arabic word şakk. There are many related payment-order documents, including bills of exchange, notes, drafts, and letters of credit, as well as specialized check forms such as counter checks, certified checks, and bank checks.

A check is considered a negotiable instrument. It instructs a bank to pay funds out of a checking account at a depository financial institution and provide those funds to the person or institution named on the check. In the United States, checks are a service provided by banks and other financial institutions that have regulatory permissions to operate demand deposit accounts, the more formal name for what we think of as checking accounts.

Today, the U.S. checking system is a highly automated means of transferring money from one party to another. Despite the fact that a checking transaction begins with a piece of paper, almost all of today's check processing is electronic. This electronic processing, combined with very high transaction volumes, keeps the per-unit cost of checking relatively low.

A customer who presents, or deposits, a check to his or her bank creates a problem for that bank. The check is a claim on an account—usually at another bank. How does the consumer's bank collect the funds from the other bank? Historically, this process, known as clearing and settlement, happened bilaterally. The deposit bank would send a messenger to the other bank; the messenger would present the check and receive funds—perhaps in gold, cash, or banknotes—in return.

Development of the checking system in the United States can be divided into three significant phases, all marked by advances in the methodology of clearing and settlement.

Phase One: The Development of Clearing Houses

In the 18th and 19th centuries in the U.S., the number of banks—and the volume of checks written on them—grew, making the process of bilateral clearing and settlement more and more cumbersome. Messengers carried bags of checks to present to other banks; the cash or other instruments received in exchange were subject to theft.

In 1853, the first check clearing house was established in New York City. Banks joined the clearing house and brought, on every banking day, deposited checks drawn on other member banks. The clearing house facilitated an orderly exchange of checks among the banks and, importantly, calculated the net settlement for each bank. The banks then funded or drew from their settlement accounts. Soon similar clearing houses were established in other major cities, as were schemes for inter-city, regional, and national exchanges of checks between clearing houses.

The Federal Reserve Bank system, formed in the early 20th century, played an important role by encouraging banks throughout the country to accept checks for deposit at par. This meant that the deposit bank would credit its customer with "one hundred cents on the dollar" rather than some lesser percentage. The Fed's successful campaign, coupled with the development of clearing houses across the country, transformed checking into a true national payments system.

What If?

If the checking system had gone in another direction, instead adopting a discount (not par) clearing and settlement model, it might have looked a lot like our interchange-based card payments system. A merchant receiving a check for $100 might deposit the check to its bank, which would credit the merchant's account for $98. The bank would then present the check to the consumer's bank, receiving $98 in credit. The consumer's bank would debit its customer's account for $100, keeping the remaining $2 as profit on the transaction.

Some industry observers have been urging the Fed to impose a similar "at par" model on debit card transactions, which are analogous to checks, with the exception of the credit and fraud guarantees provided by cards.

Phase Two: Automation—MICR and Sorters

In the late 1950s and early 1960s, the introduction and widespread use of MICR (magnetic ink character recognition) characters enabled high-speed check processing. MICR characters, identifying the bank and account a check is drawn on, appear at the bottom of a check. The check amount is added after the check is written, usually by the bank of first deposit, in a process called encoding. Check sorters, used by banks on both sides of the process and by clearing houses and processors, read the MICR line and slot the individual checks into bins. They typically also capture an image of both sides of each check as it flows through the sorter.

Other developments further enabled national-scale automated check processing. The use by depository financial institutions of a uniform bank numbering scheme—the transit routing number assigned by the American Banking Association—was an important element. The gradual dissolution of laws prohibiting interstate banking resulted in a number of large national and regional banks concentrating on a broader definition of on-us: for the first time, many banks found themselves members of multiple clearing houses. The need for long and cumbersome chains of correspondent banks for processing out-of-region checks was reduced by the advent of large scale air transportation services. Processors serving smaller banks developed "on-we" check-clearing capabilities that mimicked to some extent the multi-state check processing capabilities of national banks.

Phase Three: Imaging

While MICR and check sorting equipment automated the exchange of checks, banks still had to store paper checks. This was a particular burden on the check writer's bank, which had to keep each physical check, often returning it to its writer with the monthly statement. Others in the chain, including the deposit bank, intermediary banks, and processors, might need to see the paper check to resolve a dispute or inquiry, resulting in a tedious and costly exercise. When imaging technology began to mature in the late 1980s and 1990s, banks saw an opportunity to reduce the internal costs of storing checks and retrieving them for use in inquiries. Banks began to add cameras onto their check sorters, capturing an image of each document as it went through the machine.

Banks spent over a decade investing in and learning to use image technology, primarily for archiving purposes. Using images for clearing—exchanging images rather than paper—was a logical extension. Bankers worked together during this time, in a variety of groups, to explore "electronic checking" and "check truncation." Some banks did exchange images. Others exchanged MICR line data files for posting, with physical checks following, using private, multi-party agreements to do so. In either case, the underlying law still required that presentment to the check writer's bank be made with the original paper check. This greatly hampered efforts to clear by image, as banks anywhere along the line could need access to the original paper check in the event of a dispute, inquiry, or error.

The Check 21 law, which took effect in October 2004, solved this problem. Check 21 was proposed and sponsored by the Federal Reserve Bank, who wanted the industry to move towards electronic clearing, but did not want to mandate it.

> **Grounded Planes:** The events of September 11, 2001, are often cited as the reason for the Fed's actions in championing the Check 21 law. When planes didn't fly, and checks didn't move, for days after the attacks, the float at the Federal Reserve Bank (which technically acts as a correspondent bank in check processing: checks presented to the Fed for clearing are deposited into presenting bank's account at a Federal Reserve Bank) mounted to alarming levels, as the Fed was not able to onwardly present the checks to paying banks. In fact, the Fed had been actively working on promoting a Check 21 type of law for some time: 9/11 served as an impetus to move this forward.

Rather than mandating image clearing, the Check 21 law simply states that a printed copy of the original check (a "substitute check" or "image replacement document"—IRD) is the legal equivalent of the original paper check.

A bank may still refuse to accept images—but it must accept a printed copy of the image. Practically, this has meant that a bank of deposit, physically far removed from the check writer's bank, can send an image (usually through a clearing house) to a printer near the check writer's bank; the printout is presented on behalf of the deposit bank.

> ### Checking: Our Newest Electronic Payments System
>
> The results of Check 21 have been dramatic. Most banks began serious implementation of check image clearing in 2007. By early 2010, the Fed announced that 99% of checks clearing through the Fed were being processed electronically.

Roles and the Value Chain

The checking payments system, at its most basic, has three parties involved: the check writer, the recipient of the check, and the bank into which the check is deposited. If, as is most typical, the check writer and recipient use different banks, there are four parties. The checking value chain is illustrated in Figure 3-1.

In the checking system, it is the job of the bank of first deposit (also known as the presenting bank) to get the check to the check writer's bank (also known as the paying bank). The presenting bank will be credited by the paying bank only upon presentment of the item.

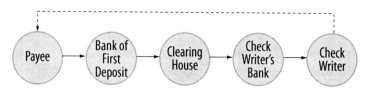

Figure 3-1.
The Checking
Value Chain

The presenting bank may present the item to the paying bank however it likes; today, it is almost always by image.

The check writer's bank offers its customer—whether a consumer, business, nonprofit, or government entity—a demand deposit account with checking as a feature. The check writer's bank provides the customer either with blank check stock or with the details (transit routing number and account number) to put on check stock that the customer provides or creates.

The check writer writes the check, specifying the payee, the date, and the dollar amount of the check. Writing may be manual, as with a consumer, or accomplished via automated printing process, as with large corporations.

The check writer then delivers the check to the recipient. The recipient deposits the check to a bank with which the recipient has a demand deposit account. (Alternatively, the recipient may endorse the check and give it to a non-bank intermediary, which then assumes the role of recipient of the check.)

> ### The Great Value of the Checking System?
>
> A little-noticed feature of checking is the fact that the check writer does not need to know, transmit, or store any information about the recipient's bank or bank account number. One could think of this as built-in PCI compliance! Of course, the check writer is sending his own account data (visible on the check), which creates another type of exposure.

The deposit bank credits the customer's account and makes the deposit available to the customer for use (such as withdrawing cash) according to its availability policy. The deposit bank's availability policy is constrained by Federal Reserve Bank Regulation CC, which dictates the minimum availability for checks of various kinds. Many banks, however, provide more generous availability terms than are required by regulation; this is a source of competition among banks, particularly for small-business deposits.

The complexity of the checking payments system is revealed at this point in the chain, when the recipient's bank, or bank of first deposit, must decide how to clear the check—that is, how to get the check to the check writer's bank.

The bank of first deposit is under no legal or regulatory constraint to clear the check in any particular way—it is free to deliver the check to the paying bank through a clearing house, through a bilateral arrangement with that bank, by depositing the check with a correspondent bank (which then becomes the "bank of second deposit"), or by turning the check over to a processor that makes the clearing decision.

The Pre-Image Clearing Environment

The Deposit Bank

A deposit bank, historically, would make these decisions by evaluating questions such as the dollar value of the check, the time of day of the deposit, distance to the paying bank, and commercial flight schedules. These factors were important because the paying bank's obligation to fund the

> ### Clearing Complexities
>
> U.C.C. 4: "A collecting bank shall send items by a reasonably prompt method, taking into consideration relevant instructions, the nature of the item, the number of those items on hand, the cost of collection involved, and the method generally used by it or others to present those items."

presentment occurred upon physical presentment of the check. The deposit bank must assess the tradeoff between getting funds faster (by delivering a check quickly) and managing delivery costs (by using a low-cost delivery mechanism). The deposit bank's presentment decision policies were input to the check sorter, which then slotted check items into bins for clearing by various methods, and to various paying banks.

The Clearing House

Most checks in the pre-imaging environment were cleared through a clearing house. A clearing house receives checks from the deposit bank, accompanied by a cash letter—basically, a deposit slip showing how many checks are being presented and for what value. Most typically, the checks brought to the clearing house are already pre-sorted into bags or bundles for each paying bank. The checks are exchanged, and the clearing house then calculates net settlement totals for the banks involved in the clearing house. A clearing house may run this settlement process itself, or may contract it out to the Federal Reserve Bank (which runs a settlement service) or other settlement provider.

> **Rendez-vous**
>
> In some cities, a "check clearing house" is little more than a place—maybe even a parking lot—where banks agree to meet to exchange bags of checks!

The Paying Bank

The paying bank receives checks from the clearing house and again runs them through a sorter, creating a file of transaction detail that is used to post transactions to check writers' accounts. Historically, these postings were done during the bank's nightly batch run of the DDA system. If, after the run, an account did not have sufficient funds to pay a check posted to the account, the paying bank could either keep the transaction and extend an overdraft loan to the customer, or reject the transaction and "bounce" it back to the presenting bank. This decision, of course, is usually automated, dictated by policies programmed into the bank's DDA system. If the bank keeps the check, and sustains the overdraft, the overdraft becomes a loan subject to the lending policies of the institution.

> **Blind Posting**
>
> Both checks and ACH debit (check-like) transactions are posted to the customer's account on what can be thought of as a "blind" basis. By this, we mean that the consumer's bank does not check, prior to the posting, whether or not there are sufficient funds in the account. There is no authorization process equivalent to that used with credit or debit cards.

Image Clearing

The Deposit Bank

In an image processing environment, the deposit bank will typically image all checks deposited payable by another bank. Where a check image is "captured" varies by bank. Highly automated banks capture most items at the point of deposit—in the ATM or at the branch teller's window. Other banks capture deposits in back-office processing centers, or deliver the paper items to a processor that handles the capture for them. The bank (or its processor) then determines whether a given item is presented under some form of bilateral arrangement with the paying bank, through some form of clearing house, or by conversion to ACH. If converted to ACH, the items must conform with NACHA rules for that transaction type.

What happens next depends very much on the deposit bank in question. It is easier to think in terms of the functions that need to occur, rather than what entities perform them. The deposit bank must:

- Deliver the images to the paying bank—either directly or through a service or processor

- Ensure that IRDs are printed out and delivered to paying banks that do not want to receive images

- Settle with the paying bank

A processor or a clearing house may handle all or some of these tasks.

Image Clearing—The Future

There are a number of scenarios under discussion, and in some cases in practice, within the industry. Immediate, dynamic presentation of a check image from an ATM (used to make a deposit) to a paying bank is one possibility. If the paying bank adopts real-time posting (rather than waiting to post during a nightly batch run), then the deposit bank would know immediately if a check bounces. Another possibility is that the image itself not be directly presented to the paying bank, but rather held in an archive accessible by either bank. In this case, the deposit bank would simply send the MICR information to the paying bank, along with the archive address, and the paying bank would post the item from this file.

> **The Impact of Image Clearing**
>
> Moving intrabank processing of check payments from paper to electronic makes a payments system that was already highly efficient even more so. The time taken to clear items has shortened dramatically, and checks now at times clear faster than ACH or cards. Perhaps most significant, the costs of transporting checks around the country have been largely eliminated. A check can now be thought of as an up-front paper order to pay—a kind of one-time payment card.

Ownership and Regulation

Ownership

No single entity owns the checking payments system. Each bank chooses how to support checking, for both checks written on its demand deposit accounts and checks deposited into its accounts. Banks usually belong to one or more check clearing houses—traditionally, bank-owned cooperatives operating on a nonprofit basis. Today, some clearing houses continue to be owned by banks, while others are owned by for-profit companies. Large processors that offer check processing to banks are similar in some functions to clearing houses.

Regulation

The regulatory framework for checking is U.S. law—specifically, the Uniform Commercial Code. Article 3 and Article 4 of the U.C.C. specifies provisions around bank deposits and collections and the liability of various parties in a checking transaction. When the U.C.C. was published in the early 1950s, and adopted by each of the 50 states, it helped to create a uniform legal framework for commercial transactions in general—and checking specifically—and reduced some legal complexities of the system. The 2004 Check 21 law was the next major U.S. law to affect checking. As previously described, Check 21 makes a substitute check (a printed copy of an image of an original check) the legal equivalent of the original.

The Federal Reserve Bank, in its role as regulator, issues regulations that implement checking law. Key Fed regulations for checking include Regulations J and CC, which together specify provisions around check availability and other aspects of check clearing. If a deposit bank is using the Federal Reserve Bank's payments services to clear checks, they are subject to the Fed's Operating Circular 3.

Check clearing houses have system rules that bind participating banks, governing presentment times, conventions for batching and cash letters, and other operational issues. Clearing house rules are not the equivalent in scope of payments system rules in card and ACH payments—they do not cover requirements for check products offered by banks to their customers. Check and image processing companies also have operations rules that are similar in scope.

> ### *Check Regulation in Transition*
>
> It is important to note that with the transition from paper-based checks to image-based checks, the laws and regulations that apply to paper checks do not apply by default to check image exchanges. This creates risk of uncertainty for all parties when disputes arise. Image exchange agreements between all the parties are the means used to address this risk..

ECCHO (Electronic Check Clearing House Organization) is a nonprofit bank cooperative (technically, a mutual benefit clearing house) that has written rules for image exchange. Banks exchanging images bilaterally, or image clearing houses, may elect to subscribe to these rules, however, these rules only apply to items exchanged among ECCHO members.

Check Use, Volumes, and Trends

Since the checking payments system is so large and decentralized, it is difficult to pinpoint volumes with any certainty. The Federal Reserve Bank periodically commissions surveys of check volumes at selected banks; these are used to project national volumes. Some such surveys look at individual items in order to determine estimates of who the payers are, who the payees are, and what the purpose of the check is.

Check volumes are very large but are declining rapidly in some segments. Data from 2001 and 2006 Fed surveys show an overall sharp decline—but particularly sharp drops in certain domains, such as point-of-sale (POS) payments and bill payment.

Checks Written (count in billions)

Type of Check	2001	2006
B2B	9.1	7.2
Payroll	8.9	5.1
Consumer POS	7	3.9
Consumer bill pay	12	11.4
P2P	5.6	2.1

Table 3-2.
Types of Checks Written
Source: Fed Studies

Some checks that are written, however, are not paid as checks, but are rather converted to ACH (see Chapter 4). Increasingly, checks that are paid as checks are cleared as images, rather than as paper.

Check Economics

The economics of the U.S. checking system can be understood by looking at check-based products sold to end parties, then at the underlying processing and clearing infrastructure that supports these products. Banks, in particular, offset costs from check-processing platforms with revenues from a number of different check products. Processing costs are changing at a dizzying rate, as the absolute volume of checks decline and, more significantly, the means of check clearing changes from paper to electronic.

Check Products

Checking Accounts—Consumers and Small Businesses

Banks offer consumers and small businesses check writing and deposit capabilities as part of bundled "checking account" products. Writing or depositing individual checks is seldom separately priced. Banks see checkwriting in particular as an essential element of a package that brings deposits to the bank. Banks do charge NSF (nonsufficient funds) fees for checks written on insufficient funds that the bank chooses not to return; historically, this has been a significant source of bank revenue. Small business checking accounts work the same way (and, in fact, typically share the same delivery platform), but often have caps on the number of checks that can be written in a given month, with transaction fees charged if the volume is exceeded. For both consumers and small businesses, banks see checking as a necessary component in an account package that brings in revenue from the value of income earned on the balance in the account, debit card interchange, and fees.

Checking Accounts—Large Enterprise

Large enterprises write many checks for payroll, benefits, and vendor payments. Banks offer checking accounts with transaction fee schedules for these enterprises. The enterprise may use the value of their "compensating balances" in their accounts to completely or partially offset the fees (called "account analysis"). A specialized checking account, called a controlled disbursement account, is used to help the enterprise understand and control the timing of checks presented for payment against the account. This information and control is important for a company wanting to optimize its use of cash, allowing better borrowing and investment decisions to be made. Positive pay fraud control (a check is paid by the bank only if it matches a check number and amount on a file provided to the bank by the enterprise) and automated account reconcilement are typical supporting services on these accounts.

Lockbox Services—Enterprises

Both banks and non-banks offer specialty products to serve enterprises that receive checks from consumers or other businesses. Retail lockbox services are designed to handle large volumes of checks from consumers (to a utility or insurance company, for example). A retail lockbox provider controls a post office box to which consumer checks are directed. The provider picks up envelops from the post office several times a day, opens the envelopes, encodes the checks, sends them into clearing, scans the remittance advice (which the consumer has put into the envelope with the check), and creates a file of payments received for the enterprise customer to use in updating its billing files. This is a highly automated and historically low-margin business. The value proposition to the enterprise customer is accelerated collection of funds and automated data capture. Pricing is on a per-transaction basis, with additional charges for data feeds, etc.

Wholesale lockbox services are similar, but focus on high-value checks received from business customers. The incoming remittance advices are each different (the format is determined by the paying customer's check-printing system) and the process of capturing data from them is less automated and more expensive. The value of wholesale lockbox traditionally is heavily dependent on faster clearing of high-value checks—automated data capture is secondary.

Image clearing and remote deposit check capture are significantly changing the dynamics of this business. Many wholesale lockbox providers now handle inbound ACH payments and inbound checks, creating a single point of information about bank deposits and remittance data feeds. Pricing is on a per-transaction and often per-keystroke-entered basis, with additional charges for data feeds.

Remote Deposit Capture

Remote deposit capture (RDC) products are offered by banks and non-banks to enterprises of all sizes. This service, shown in Figure 3-2, allows the enterprise to scan and electronically deposit a check it receives.

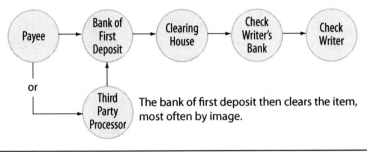

Remote deposit capture is a product offered to a payee, most typically a small or medium-sized merchant or other business. The payee captures an image of the check and electronically "deposits" it—either to the payee's bank or to a third-party processor, which then deposits it.

The bank of first deposit then clears the item, most often by image.

Figure 3-2.
Remote Deposit Capture

The RDC provider assumes the risk that the enterprise has scanned a valid paper check. If the provider is a non-bank, the image is deposited in a bank. Iin either case, the bank can then submit it for clearing as an image or, at its option, convert it to a substitute check and clear it as paper. The value proposition to the enterprise is the time and costs saved by not physically depositing the check. Providers are becoming more flexible regarding the scanning devices supported for the service. Some banks are beginning to introduce RDC for consumers as well, and some of these support the use of common home scanners. Remote deposit capture is typically priced on a flat per-transaction basis.

Retail Merchant Check Deposit Services

Large retail merchants have historically received high volumes of checks in payment for purchases. Unlike billers, merchants must make an acceptance decision at the point of payment. Many retailers use automated systems to decide whether or not to accept a check, based on reading the MICR line at an ECR (electronic cash register) or a terminal with check reading capabilities. The decision system may simply use data from the retailer's internal system (a file of known bad-check writers, for example), or may access external databases. A retailer may opt to have the check verified (determining if the account is real and in good standing), or even guaranteed, by service providers offering these options. Most large retailer systems encode checks as received (put the dollar amount on the MICR line) to avoid bank charges for doing so. The retailer pays a per-transaction deposit fee to the bank or the non-bank party accepting the transaction. If the retailer is using a check guarantee service, the provider charges a fixed fee plus percent of value charge; this makes the economics of the transaction similar to those of credit card acceptance.

Retail merchants need to determine if checks received will be converted to ACH and, if so, whether they will be converted at the cash register (POP, or Point of Purchase format) or in the back office (BOC, or Back Office Conversion format), converted to image (remote deposit capture), or deposited as paper. NACHA rules place restrictions on what types of checks may be converted. Some retailers do this in house. Others turn the checks over to a service provider that makes the decisions, and processes and deposits transactions, on their behalf.

Other Check Products—Consumers

Consumers buy (or are given) blank checkbooks from either their banks or third-party check printers—companies that also supply banks with check stock.

Unbanked consumers use check equivalents offered by non-banks. Check cashing services allow consumers to cash checks by endorsing the check over to the service. Money orders are sold by stores, the post office, and other retail service providers.

There are also a number of specialty consumer checking products, including traveler's checks, certified checks, cashier's checks, and bank checks.

Other Check Products—Enterprises

Many small businesses write checks using accounting software packages (for example, QuickBooks); the software companies and other providers supply check stock to work with these packages.

Some large enterprises print checks in house, using a check printer that receives its data feed from the enterprise's accounts payable and/or payroll system. Others outsource the process to check printing services. This is particularly common for payroll applications, with the service managing multiple aspects of payroll (tax calculations, etc.). Such services also manage the enterprise's ACH payroll payments.

Check Clearing and Infrastructure Economics

Banks, clearing houses, and processors all participate in the economic value chain for check clearing. Banks generally have separate operational areas to handle check deposit processing and "in-clearing," the process of receiving checks presented to the bank for payment. Either or both of these areas may be outsourced to a processor.

The bank or processor has operational expenses associated with accepting or delivering paper checks; operating check sorters; imaging and archiving checks; running and maintaining the applications that apply bank policy to individual items to determine check posting times, funds availability, and overdrafts; and managing the reconcilement of settlement accounts. Clearing houses have expenses associated with determining settlement totals, and managing the settlement process.

Processors and clearing houses charge transaction fees to banks that use their services. Many banks provide correspondent services to smaller banks: the bigger bank may act as a processor and handle check processing, again on a transaction-fee basis, but with an account analysis factor (giving the smaller bank credit for the value of balances held at its bank).

In general, banks and processors have significant expenses associated with bounced checks and exception items; these costs can greatly exceed the cost of "normal" items. Banks use the expression "Day 2 Processing" to refer to all activities (returns, adjustments, statement rendering, research, etc.) resulting after acceptance or refusal of an item by the paying bank.

A final, important element of check economics—for all parties—is the cost of fraud, and of fraud (and other risk) management.

What is Float? (Part 2 of 2)

Float is an integral part of the economics of the checking system, and also one of the most misunderstood terms in the business! This is partly because the term is used in multiple ways. In the abstract, float refers to a gap in the availability of funds transferred between two parties. Sometimes this is concrete: "Federal Reserve float" occurs when the Fed, acting as a check clearing house, credits a deposit bank for funds received, prior to collecting from the paying bank. (Historically, the Fed has done this as a way to manage, on behalf of the presenting bank, uncertainties in check collection.) Often float is more a matter of perception: "disbursement float" is a term used to describe the gap between when a corporation mails a check (and presumably discharges its obligation to a vendor) and the time that the check is actually presented to its bank for payment. Float is often discussed in relative terms: if a bank has been collecting deposited checks on an average of 1.5 days after receipt, and it reduces that to an average of 1.25 days, it has improved float. If a bank makes good funds available to a depositing customer prior to receiving payment on the check in question, it is incurring a float expense—which may be theoretical, rather than actual, if the customer in question leaves the balances in the account. Confused? Here's one thing to remember about float. Image clearing, and related products and concepts (ACH check conversion, remote deposit capture), are greatly reducing the amount—and importance—of float in the U.S. checking system.

Risk Management

Check fraud has a long and colorful history. It falls into many categories, including forged checks; forged signatures on legitimate checks; altered amounts, dates, or payees; fraudulent endorsement; and scheme frauds such as check kiting. Writing a check on insufficient funds in an account (called NSF), while technically fraud, is generally seen as a separate category of risk exposure.

NSF Risk

The payee accepting a check is exposed to the risk of the check "bouncing." If the check writer's bank pays the check on insufficient funds, the risk of collecting from the consumer moves to the bank (as does the revenue from an NSF fee to the consumer!). When a bounced check is returned, the depository bank debits its customer's account; if that customer has since drained the funds from the account, that bank is at risk. Payees (or their banks) may re-present a bounced check for payment, either as paper, by image, or via an ACH transaction. As discussed above, payees, particularly retailers, may use internal or external databases or services to help manage this risk. Payees may also choose to purchase check verification or guarantee services.

Retail merchants, billers, and enterprises are the most exposed to NSF risk. Industry estimates of annual losses are in the range of $10 billion, though no precise figures are known. Bank losses to NSF are not disclosed, but are much smaller. Banks, in general, find these losses acceptable given the very lucrative NSF fee revenue collected from their consumers.

Check Fraud

If a check is forged on a valid account, or a valid check is altered, and a payee accepts this and deposits it, someone is going to lose money on the fraud. The check writer's bank has a legal obligation to pay an item when it is "properly payable"; the check writer, like the other parties, has a responsibility to exercise "ordinary care." Provisions in the U.C.C. as well as a significant amount of case law result in major losses due to fraud being allocated by the courts—or by arbitration—to various parties to the transaction. Determining exposure is complex, particularly given the transition to imaging and subsequent regulatory complications. Practically speaking, merchants (and billers) end up with quite a bit of exposure, as do check writing corporations. Merchant losses due to bounced checks are believed to be significantly higher than from other types of check fraud. In the U.S., bank exposure to check fraud is generally believed to be less than $1 billion annually.

Counterfeit checks (including counterfeit cashier's checks) are drawn on nonexistent accounts. Such checks become the responsibility of the depository bank, which then attempts to reclaim funds from the depositing customer's account.

Risk Management Products

To help minimize fraud, retailers buy check verification and guarantee products, as discussed above, as well as access to external databases. Banks buy similar products to guide the decision to accept a check for deposit and cashing; the banking industry collaborates on a database, administered by Early Warning Services, that provides this data. Bank processors provide software that helps identify fraudulent transactions by examining patterns of transactions within and across accounts. (Similar software is used to detect transactions that violate money-laundering regulation.) Banks and retailers use a wide range of products and services to detect check forgeries, identify fraudulent signatures, etc.

Major Providers

The Federal Reserve Bank

The Federal Reserve Board and the Federal Reserve Banks (together, "the Fed") have a unique position in the checking industry. "The Fed" plays three roles:

- As a payments industry regulator, it writes the rules that govern practices by banks and other parties across multiple payments systems.

- As a provider of payments services, it operates the largest check and check image clearing houses in the country. (It also operates one of the two ACH switches and one of the two wire transfer systems

(Fedwire), and is the sole provider of cash and currency to banks.) The Fed sells these services only to banks.

- As the manager of the National Net Settlement system, it provides settlement services to multiple private sector clearing houses, both paper and electronic.

The Clearing House

The Clearing House, a national bank-owned payments company, is a quiet powerhouse in the banking industry. Originally the New York Clearing House (for check clearing), established in 1853, it grew through a series of mergers with other clearing houses and payments companies, and through establishing new payments services to serve its member banks. Today it is owned by twenty large banks (both U.S. banks and the U.S. branches of international banks). It is a major competitor to the Fed in providing payments services to banks—offering check and image clearing, ACH processing (it's the one other ACH operator in the country), and, through CHIPs, wire transfer processing.

Banks	Hardware & Software
Clearing Houses/Networks	IBM
The Fed	NCR
The Clearing House	Unisys
Viewpointe	
Processors	**Services**
FIS Global	Certegy, DebitBureau, ChexSystems (FIS Global)
Fiserv	TeleCheck (First Data)
Jack Henry	Carreker (Fiserv)
Harland Financial	NCN (Intuit)
Groups	Wausau Financial Services
ECCHO	Net Deposit
ABA	Endpoint Exchange
Not all providers or all categories are listed.	

Table 3-3.
Major Industry Providers—
Checking

Summary: Checking

Checking, long the dominant non-cash payments system in the U.S., is in decline. But radical changes in check clearing practices have transformed the economics of the system—and there may be reason to think that checking will find a new life in the decades to come.

Key Trends in Checking

- Check volumes are still very large, but are dropping overall, and most sharply in POS and bill payment domains.

- Image clearing and check-to-ACH conversion have drastically changed bank clearing practices and the unit cost of handling checks.

- Remote image capture by ATMs, branches, and end parties is lowering the cost of check acceptance, and reducing float and risk.

- Card ISOs are bundling check acceptance and validation/guaranty services with card acceptance for retail merchants.

- Working groups are looking at "fully electronic checks" (one possible term - EPO, or electronic payment order) - an instrument that starts life as a check image.

Sources of Information—Checking

- ECCHO
- The Clearing House
- The Federal Reserve Bank
- Federal Reserve Board of Governors (staff papers)
- Retail Payments Office
- Individual Federal Reserve Banks
- Financial Services Technology Consortium
- Bank Administration Institute (BAI)

Core Systems: ACH

Overview—ACH	
Type	**Push and pull payments**
Ownership	Owned by banks
Regulation	NACHA rules and Federal Reserve Bank regulation
Network Economics	Clears at par
Processing	Electronic
Risk Management	Left to intermediaries and end parties. ACH Operators provide some risk management at the network level.

Table 4-1.
ACH Overview

History and Background

The ACH, or Automated Clearing House, is one of the largest payments network in the United States. It is a bank-owned utility used for many different types of consumer and enterprise applications.

The ACH system was started in the 1970s by bankers working in check processing. With the introduction of check reader/sorters, it became obvious that all that was required to post transactions to customer accounts was the MICR data. "Why not," these bankers asked, "simply exchange MICR data directly, rather than exchanging checks and then extracting the MICR data?" Note that this was *not* an early attempt at check truncation or check image clearing—it focused on having the electronic transaction replace the paper transaction entirely.

Note:

To really understand the ACH system, first read Chapter 3, Checking. The ACH was created by the people who ran checking operations in banks.

Bankers focused, in the early days of ACH, on high-volume, low-risk, repetitive transactions—particularly payroll checks, social security benefit checks, and insurance premium payments.

The result is that the ACH, more than any other payments network in the United States, is wired in to every demand deposit account in the country. An enterprise wishing to make or collect a payment using one of the ACH transaction types can do so, and safely plan on being able to reach every banked consumer and enterprise in the country. (In addition, consumers holding network-branded prepaid cards (see Chapter 5) can have funds deposited into those card accounts by the ACH.)

Roles and the Value Chain

As background to this section, it is important to understand that the ACH is the *only* payments system that handles both push and pull payments transactions:

• **A push transaction** (referred to as an ACH Credit) is initiated by the payer of funds, and sends money to the receiving party.

• **A pull transaction** (referred to as an ACH Debit) is initiated by the receiver of funds, and pulls money from the paying party.

The basic roles, and the core value chain, are the same for both push and pull payments—as shown in Figure 4-1—though, as we will see, the risks and economics are quite different for each type.

> ### Cracking the Chicken and Egg Problem
>
> The fledgling ACH network was formed in the early 1970s. It was designed to keep costs low for participating banks. In most parts of the country, local ACH associations were formed by bankers participating in each area's check clearing house. But participation was still optional and, in the early days, the network faced the same "chicken and egg" problem faced by all new payments networks. For the ACH, the question was, "How do we get consumers to sign up for ACH (say, for direct deposit of payroll) if most banks don't participate? And how do we get banks to participate if we don't have consumers asking to be paid this way?" The answer, in this case, was the government. The U.S. government offered to pay Social Security benefits via ACH. It asked banks, in effect, "Do you have any customers who receive social security benefits?" The answer, of course, was yes—and over a period of 15 years virtually all "depository financial institutions," including thrifts, savings and loans, and credit unions, joined the ACH network.

In the ACH system, an **originator** delivers transactions to its bank. Each bank in the system chooses an operator. The operator sorts and forwards the transactions to receiving banks or other operators.

The ACH Value Chain

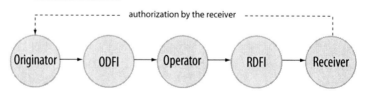

The flow is exactly the same for both push and pull transactions. The originator is responsible for obtaining the receiver's authorization for the transaction. The ODFI is liable to the network for the actions of its originator clients.

Figure 4-1.
The ACH Value Chain

An ACH transaction is entered into the ACH payments system by an origi-nator, most typically an enterprise. The originator delivers the transaction to its bank, called the ODFI, or originating depository financial institution. The ODFI credits or debits its customer's account (depending whether the transaction is pull or push) and forwards the transaction to its chosen ACH operator. The operator performs a switch role, passing the transactions on to the RDFI, or receiving depository financial institution. (If the ODFI and the RDFI use different ACH operators, the first operator switches the trans-action to the second operator.) The RDFI then debits or credits the account of its customer (the recipient), again depending on whether the transaction is pull or push.

ACH Settlement

Today, ACH operators calculate net settlement totals for their banks on a daily basis. These totals are submitted to the Fed, which manages the actual settlement process using its National Settlement Service. Practically speak-ing, this results in "zero float" among the banks and their clients—although some banks may manage debits or credits to client accounts in order to accommodate risk policies.

In 2009, the Fed, in its role as an ACH operator, announced a plan to provide "same-day" settlement. One of the moti-vations was to ensure that a check converted to ACH for-mat would not have a longer settlement time than if it were cleared as an image—which can clear on the same day. The Fed also hopes that this will enable better risk management through faster posting of returns. This option is limited to certain types of ACH transactions, currently including check conversions, but also customer initiated and WEB and TEL transac-tions. During the introductory phase of the service, RDFIs will have to opt in to the service to participate.

> **Faster Payments**
>
> In the U.K., the banks have implemented a new payments system, "Faster Payments," which acts like the ACH (electronic, batch) but processes on a same-day basis. It is used for push payments, particularly bill-pay transactions.

Ownership and Regulation

The ACH is owned, in effect, by the banks (depository financial institutions) that belong to it. NACHA (originally the National Automated Clearing House Association, now NACHA—The Electronic Payments Association) is a nonprofit association that oversees the network. Depository financial institutions (referred to here as "banks") belong to NACHA either directly or through a local or regional payments association. The NACHA bylaws govern how voting power is allocated among both types of members.

NACHA's Role

NACHA's primary role is rule-making, discussed below. Unlike the card networks, NACHA is not involved in processing. Transaction switching among the intermediary banks is done by an ACH operator. (Currently, there are only two operators—the Federal Reserve Bank and EPN, owned by The Clearing House.)

NACHA is actively involved with its member institutions, and their corporate clients, in developing and testing product enhancements and new products. It does not, however, operate on the same scale as the card networks. It has a significantly lower budget than the networks, and so can't develop new products and distribute them through member banks.

> It will be interesting to observe how the brand question plays out in the eCommerce domain. Today, we see third party brands appearing alongside the card brands on checkout pages, but if a merchant accepts ACH "eChecks", they are apt to put a descriptor such as "pay with your bank account".

Neither does NACHA play a role in brand creation or communication. In this way, it is more similar to the check clearing houses than to the card networks. Although some "small b" brands have evolved ("direct deposit of payroll", and, arguably, "eCheck"), there is no ACH equivalent of an acceptance mark such as "Visa" or "NYCE". Despite this lack, the system has shown robust growth, by providing an efficient set of "rails" for banks and their customers to use.

The ACH system has no end-party brands similar to those in the card payments systems. Some "small-b" brands (e.g., direct deposit of payroll) have been established through common usage. Other terms (e.g., eCheck) have not yet achieved that status.

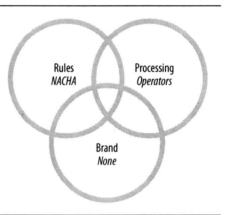

Figure 4-2.
ACH—Where's the Brand?

ACH Regulation

ACH transactions are governed both by private, NACHA rules, and by Federal Reserve Bank regulation.

The NACHA rules bind the ODFIs, the RDFIs, and the ACH operators. Originators, receivers, and third-party service providers are bound by contractual agreements with their ODFIs and/or RDFIs. NACHA rules are voted on by members of NACHA: the larger banks, which belong directly to NACHA, and the regional associations, who represent smaller banks through their membership in NACHA.

ACH rules specify some of the provisions of these downstream contracts, and fall into three groups:

- Rules that apply to all ACH transactions

- Rules that apply to ACH Debit (pull) transactions or ACH Credit (push) transactions

- Rules that apply to only certain ACH types, defined by the Standard Entry Class Code

ACH operators have private rules that bind ODFIs and RDFIs using their services. These rules are very narrow in scope relative to the ACH rules. For example, banks that use the Federal Reserve Bank as an operator are subject to Operating Circular 4.

In addition to these private rules, U.S. law applies to many types of ACH transactions:

- Regulation E of the Federal Reserve Bank, implementing the Electronic Funds Transfer Act, applies to consumer transactions. Regulation E is the key regulation that specifies consumers' right to return unauthorized transactions.

- U.C.C. 4 and 4a apply to ACH corporate credit transfers.

- Federal government ACH transactions are regulated by the Treasury Department.

> ### Why ACH is Different
>
> Why is NACHA's role so limited, when the ACH network is so pervasive? The answer—of course—is money. Banks using the ACH network do not pay a "tax" to NACHA (comparable to the card network assessments). As a result, NACHA does not have the resources for product development, brand advertising, or network expansion that the card networks do. One could argue, of course, that the reason the card networks can charge such a "tax" is because of the direct revenues (interest, interchange, fees) that the banks earn on issuing card products.

If there is a conflict in rules, obviously, U.S. law prevails over private association rules. This means that NACHA must ensure that any new U.S. law or regulation is either correctly reflected in the ACH rules, or at least not contradicted. This has become increasingly complex—partly because of check-to-ACH conversion, and partly because of increasingly expansive federal law and regulation around consumer rights.

ACH Use, Volumes, and Trends

The ACH system is broadly used for many types of payments. Both large and small enterprises, including corporations, governments, and nonprofits, use the ACH to make payments to, and to collect payments from, consumers. Enterprises also use the ACH to make payments to each other, and to transfer funds within a company. In the card payments systems, merchant acquirers use ACH to credit merchants with funds from their card payment activity.

ACH volumes have grown steadily since inception. In recent years, there has been particularly strong growth of the WEB transaction type in particular.

B2C	B2B	eChecks
PPD Credit—(Direct Deposit) Preauthorized Payroll, Benefits	CCD Debit	Consumer-initiated
		WEB
	CCD Credit	TEL
		POS
PPD Debit—Preauthorized Debits		Check Conversion
	CTX	ARC
		POP
		BOC
		RCK

Table 4-2.
ACH Transaction Types

ACH transactions are classified with transaction codes, called SECs or Standard Entry Codes, specifying transaction type. The SEC transaction code is included in every transaction, giving the ACH system detail about the uses of the system that some other payments systems cannot offer. A full list of SEC codes is available through NACHA. Table 4-2 lists common ACH transaction types.

Primary Uses of the ACH System

Preauthorized consumer transactions

PPD (prearranged payment and deposit) Credit transactions are used for payroll, pension, and benefit payments to consumers. PPD Debit transactions are used primarily for recurring bill payments from consumers. These two transaction types built early volume for the ACH, and growth in both categories has been steady over its history. Both require consumers to preauthorize transactions.

> **Risk Management**
>
> A business paying its supplier by ACH has the burden of collecting and maintaining the supplier's bank account information. On the other hand, the paying company is not revealing its own bank account data, as it does when sending a check.

Business-to-business transactions

CCD (corporate credit or debit) Credit transactions are used for supplier payments, in lieu of checks. CCD Debit transactions may also be used for supplier payments—for example, when a corporate customer gives a trusted supplier the ability to debit its account. When suppliers are paid with CCD transactions, the customer frequently must send remittance data (explaining details of the payment) separately by mail, fax, or email.

CCD Debit transactions are frequently used for intracompany funds concentration. A corporation with bank accounts in multiple states, for example, may use the ACH to pull funds into a single account for investment. CCD Debits are also used for government tax collections.

CTX (corporate trade exchange) Credit transactions are similar to those via CCD Credit, but are designed to carry addenda records with each financial transaction. This allows a corporate customer to pay a supplier and send re-mittance data along with the payment; the RDFI is required to provide the data it receives to the receiving corporation.

Although checks remain the predominant form of supplier payments in the United States, business-to-business ACH transactions have grown steadily. One challenge is that the paying enterprise must collect and maintain bank account information (transit routing number and account number) for each supplier it pays electronically—a process not required when paying by check.

Check conversion transactions

Beginning in 2001, NACHA, in cooperation with the Federal Reserve Bank (in its regulatory role with respect to Regulation E), approved a series of new ACH transaction codes to implement check conversion. The permit-ted situations vary by category listed below, but have certain parameters in common. As shown in Figure 4-3, each transaction begins when someone writes a paper check. When that check is given to the payee, the payee, in cooperation with its bank, creates a new ACH transaction to replace the check. The original check is destroyed and the ACH transaction is carried through the ACH network to effect a debit at the check writer's bank. The payment ceases being governed by check law and regulation, and is instead governed by ACH rules and regulation.

The ARC service is offered to a biller by its lockbox bank. Checks are scanned, and an ACH file created from MICR line data and the dollar amount. The ACH debit transaction is forwarded to the bank's ACH operator. The check is destroyed after a brief retention period.

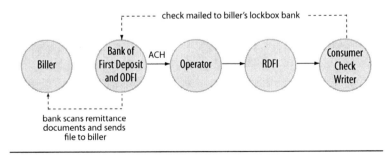

Figure 4-3.
ACH Check Conversion

- **ARC (accounts receivable conversion)** transactions occur when a consumer check is received at a bank lockbox that is serving a biller.

With the agreement of the biller, the check is converted to an ACH transaction. The consumer is notified passively (by, for example, a notice in a statement "stuffer"); the consumer's positive consent is not required.

- **POP (point of purchase)** transactions occur when a consumer check is presented at a cash register point of sale. The clerk takes the check, runs it through the register to capture the MICR data, and returns the check to the consumer, stamped as void. The register then generates the ACH transaction to debit the consumer's account. (The POP transaction, not surprisingly, created some initial confusion among consumers—"Why am I getting my check back?")

- **BOC (back-office conversion)** transactions occur when a consumer provides a check at either a point of sale or a biller location. As the name implies, the actual conversion occurs not in front of the consumer, but in the originator's (or ODFI's) back office. Notice to the consumer that BOC will occur must be posted at the point of sale or other check-receiving location.

- **RCK (represented check entry)** is used when a bank represents a "bounced" check with an ACH.

DCT (depository check truncation) is a pilot program to allow banks to clear low-value checks in ACH format.

Most business-to-business checks and government-to-consumer checks are not yet eligible for conversion to ACH.

Ad hoc consumer transactions

This group of transactions is the focus of much interest in the payments community. Although, like the check conversion transactions above, they are often referred to as "eChecks", these transactions do not start as checks—they start as "native electronic" ACH transactions. The important difference between these transactions and the PPD debit transactions described above is that, as the name implies, consumers do not preauthorize ad hoc transactions with an assumption of ongoing use. Rather, they can be used for one-time consumer transactions, as well as recurring transactions. The consumer's authorization is still very important, particularly since these transactions (like all ACH consumer debit transactions) are covered by ACH rules and Reg E provisions, which ensure that a consumer can refuse an unauthorized transaction.

On its website, the biller offers the consumer an option to pay "using your bank account." The consumer enters his or her bank routing and account numbers and authorizes the transaction.

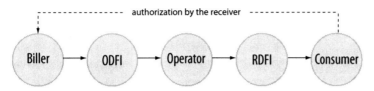

The biller is liable for the validity of this authorization; the consumer's right to repudiate unauthorized transactions is mandated by Federal Reserve Board Regulation E. The ODFI is responsible to the network for the biller's compliance. The biller, of course, is also subject to good-funds risk, as the debit may "bounce" for insufficient funds.

Figure 4-4.
ACH WEB Transactions

An ACH WEB transaction, as shown in Figure 4-4, is authorized by a consumer, over the Internet. Its primary uses are bill payment, eCommerce purchases, and account-to-account transfers. A consumer making an online payment is shown an option such as "pay from your bank account"; he or she then enters a bank routing number and account number. The biller or merchant, in the role of originator, then takes a batch of similar transactions and passes them to its ODFI.

Mechanically, this is the same process used for any ACH debit transaction. The potential risks are considerably higher, however: a consumer could enter another person's bank account information, and the fraud (or error) might not be caught until that other person saw the incorrect debit on his or her bank account. Reg E establishes a "60 days from date of statement receipt" window for the consumer to repudiate the debit—effectively putting the ODFI, and its originator customer, at risk for up to 90 days. Despite this potential risk, actual return rates on WEB transactions are quite low, apparently evidencing sound work on authenticating the transactions on the part of the originator and the ODFI.

WEB transactions are also used by third-party payments services such as PayPal. Typically, the third-party payment service structures a two-part payment. As an example, consider an eCommerce purchase. The payment service pays the eCommerce merchant directly; most typically, this is an ACH credit transaction in which the payment service is the originator. The second transaction occurs when the

> ### *Who Controls the ACH?*
>
> Although banks control ACH rules (by voting, directly or through membership in regional ACH associations), at times it has seemed that rules are approved which are contrary to bank interests. Most dramatically, the 2001 approval of the WEB transaction code, which enabled a highly successful large-scale migration of bill payments from check to electronics—also enabled an unanticipated and arguably bank-unfriendly use of the system. Third-party payments services providers, most notably PayPal, used the transaction code to pull inexpensive ACH debit transactions to fund eCommerce purchases by their customers. This meant, in some situations, that the ACH transaction took the place of what would have been a more profitable debit card transaction for the consumer's bank. This has been the source of some controversy in the industry. As a result, bankers responsible for ACH rule decisions have become increasingly cautious, hoping to avoid additional encounters with the "laws of unintended consequences."

payment service, again acting as originator, submits a WEB debit transaction to pull funds from the consumer's account.

The third party in the example above is at extreme risk if the consumer transaction is fraudulent—e.g., if the consumer has given someone else's bank account information. To manage this risk, PayPal early on developed a "micro deposit" scheme designed to verify account ownership. By making two small, random deposits in the consumer's bank account, and then asking the consumer to report the amounts, PayPal can verify that the consumer is the valid owner of that bank account. Other users of WEB transactions have followed PayPal in this approach to verification. This tactic protects the originator (and therefore the ODFI) from most fraud risk but does not, of course, cover the NSF risk.

TEL transactions are similar to WEB transactions, but allow the consumer to provide authorization over the telephone. TEL transactions are most commonly used for consumer bill payment.

The POS transaction type is still small in terms of transaction volume, but holds a great deal of promise—and interest—in the payments community. Here, the consumer is not remote, but present at a physical point of sale. The merchant, acting as an originator, creates one-time consumer debit transaction. The merchant must obtain consumer authorization, and faces the same challenge in verifying bank account information. Merchants (and third-party payment providers) use a wide range of authentication schemes, many involving cards (a payment-enabling supermarket loyalty card, for example, or a driver's license), biometrics, or mobile phones.

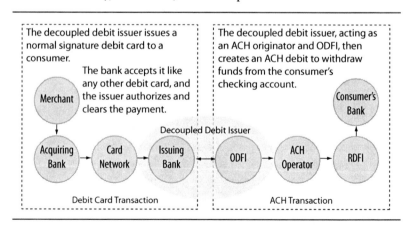

Figure 4-5.
Decoupled Debit

International Transactions

Although the ACH system is not international, both ACH operators and the ACH rules support the concept of links between ACH and other payments systems. Some early users were corporations paying retirees or employees in other countries. The Fed, acting as an ACH operator, established links to countries such as Canada and the U.K. to handle credit (push) payments. Businesses also began to use these links for cross-border supplier payments. Because these types of transactions involve more than one payments system, considerable difficulties are associated with timing, risk management, settlement (especially foreign exchange management), and data formats. Increasing attention has been given to the need to comply with laws, in the U.S. and other jurisdictions, designed to combat money laundering and other criminal activities. In 2009, NACHA implemented a new transaction code, IAT (international ACH transaction) to label and to enable appropriate management and compliance of such international transactions.

Economics

The ACH system was designed as a low-cost, widely used utility for banks and their customers. It has largely succeeded in that goal: the cost, for enterprises and consumers, of using the system is very low, as is the cost, to bankers and processors, of providing the system. There is no interchange in the ACH system, and no float or lending revenue directly related to it.

ACH Products

ACH Origination

Banks and third parties compete for corporate ACH origination business, including payroll, preauthorized debits, business-to-business transactions, and the various eChecks. Large corporations transmit batch files of transactions to their ODFIs; both small and large corporations may also execute smaller numbers of ACH transactions over online systems provided by a bank or a third party.

> #### Bank and Non-bank Competition
> Banks and non-banks often compete. When a non-bank offers ACH services to a client, that non-bank (or its client) must have an arrangement with a bank to act as ODFI and/or RDFI.

Total fee and fee equivalent revenue to banks for origination is considerably less than the revenue associated, for example, with credit card issuance. Pricing to corporate originators varies by size of enterprise and type of transaction. A very high-volume payroll file, for example, might be priced at pennies per transaction. A lower-volume B2B transaction might be priced at 50 cents or a dollar per transaction.

ACH origination is often sold as part of a package of specialized services, such as these:

- **Payroll.** Banks and third parties compete to provide payroll services to enterprises of all sizes. Services often include management of tax calculations and withholdings as well as check issuance, ACH origination, and employee reporting and service.

- **Retail lockbox.** Banks and third parties compete to manage inbound consumer bill payments by check. The same entities often support receipt of preauthorized ACH payments for bill payment, and the conversion of checks received into ACH ARC (accounts receivable) debits.

- **Wholesale lockbox.** Banks and third parties compete to manage inbound business remittances by check, ACH, and wire. Remittance data handling is a key part of this service—it may include manual data entry (for remittance data coming with checks) and reformatting of data received with ACH transactions. To date, there is little conversion to ACH of business-to-business checks.

- **Supplier payments.** Banks and third parties compete to handle outbound business remittances to suppliers. These services may include printing checks and associated remittance data, preparing ACH transactions, and managing outbound remittance data through a variety of channels, including ACH (CTX), mail, fax, email, transmission to third-party VANs, etc. More advanced services could include collection and management of electronic invoices or maintenance of supplier databases.

- **Retail payment acceptance.** Banks, card acquirers, and other third parties compete to offer services to retailers receiving checks at the point of sale. These services may include conversion of the check to an ACH item or presentment of the check by image. Item verification or guarantee may be part of this offering. As point-of-sale ACH services mature, it is logical that the same providers will offer this service to merchants.

Banks and third parties often incorporate ACH origination into a package of services, bundled with value-added services (e.g., state tax calculations sold along with payroll payments).

ACH Receipt

Banks and third parties rarely charge their customers for receipt of an ACH transaction, i.e., for acting as an RDFI. There are some exceptions, particularly for B2B transactions.

ACH Expenses

Bank Processing and Clearing

Banks tend to run ACH operations centers as cost centers that support multiple areas of the bank—both the consumer accounts organization, for example, and the corporate payments organization might use the same ACH "engine." Medium and large banks buy specialized software that allows them to process both ACH originations and receipts. Smaller banks may outsource part or all of their ACH operations to processors.

Banks remove on-us ACH transactions submitted by originators and post those transactions directly to the receiver's account. The bank then sends the remaining origination transactions to its ACH operator, which sorts the transactions and sends them on to either the RDFI (if both use the same operator) or to another operator as appropriate. Operators charge for both receipt and delivery of ACH batches—costs are dependent on volume, but at high volumes are in fractions of a penny per transaction.

Historically, bank ACH operations were relatively inexpensive to run, particularly when most transactions were preauthorized consumer debits and credits. For banks, the proliferation of new transaction types, each with its own risk management and compliance considerations, has increased the cost of managing the ACH process—offset, in part, by revenue from new services and products.

One challenging element is the RDFI's management of disputed consumer transactions. The RDFI receives no compensation for an inbound PPD Debit or WEB transaction. If a consumer disputes a transaction, the RDFI bears the costs of managing the dispute—which can often exceed the value of the transaction itself. (This process also occurs in checking—but banks have found the electronic ACH process simpler and less costly.)

> ### ACH Economics—Under the Interchange Umbrella
>
> Merchants, billers, and other receivers receiving most payment via credit or debit card are used to paying a merchant discount fee—a blend of fixed and percentage costs determined in large part by the card network's interchange fee schedule. For such receivers of funds, ACH offers the opportunity for a dramatic cost reduction. An eCommerce merchant selling a $100 item might pay $2.50 in discount fees if a credit card is used, vs. perhaps pennies if an ACH eCheck is used. Against this economic benefit, the merchant would have to weigh the cost of risk management: will the transaction be denied by the consumer as fraudulent, or will the transaction bounce for insufficient funds? At least two economic models are being formed for such ACH transactions: one in which the receiver (merchant or biller) bears those risks, and one in which a third party assumes some or all of the risk for the recipient. If a third party bears risk, the cost of the transaction to the merchant will, of course, go up.

Risk Management

Users and providers of ACH services are exposed to a number of risks that must be managed:

- ODFIs are liable for the actions of their originating clients. In particular, authorization from the underlying receiver is often the responsibility of the originator; this responsibility is carried to the ODFI. This is critically important with ACH debit (pull) transactions. If either the identity of the underlying receiver is wrong (for example, A uses B's name fraudulently) or the bank account information is wrong (B gives C's bank account information by mistake), the ODFI is financially responsible. Obviously, an ODFI will pass on that responsibility to the originator in its contract; however, if the originator is a small or financially unstable company, it may not be able to repay the ODFI.

- RDFIs must accurately post transactions. If the transaction is an ACH debit (pull) transaction, the RDFI must handle returns for NSF or disputed transactions according to a specified timeline.

- Merchants and billers originating ACH debits must manage the risk that transactions will be returned for NSF or, for consumer transactions, for lack of authorization—this latter dispute can happen as late as 60 days after the consumer's receipt of a statement or notification from his or her bank.

- Businesses must carefully manage bank accounts to ensure that no fraudulent ACH debit transactions are posted (as they must with checks as well). Importantly, a business receiving an unauthorized ACH debit does not have the Reg E protections that a consumer has.

Major Providers

Because of the reach of the ACH system, there is a large ecosystem of providers who are involved in some way in ACH origination, receipt, or processing. Many bank and processors embed ACH capabilities in with other payments products.

- **NACHA** sets, develops, and enforces adherence to ACH rules and handles much of the definition of new product and transaction types. NACHA balances the needs of small financial institutions—some of which are only RDFIs—with the needs of larger ODFIs.

- **The Federal Reserve Bank** is pivotal in ACH, playing three roles: as regulator, as one of the two large-scale ACH operators, and as the provider of settlement services.

Banks—Large ODFIs		Networks	
JPMorgan Chase		NACHA	
Wells Fargo		Regional associations	
Bank of America			
Citibank		**Software & Services**	
		FiServ	
Operators		FIS	
The Fed		First Data	
The Clearing House (EPN)		ACI	

Not all providers or all categories are listed.

Table 4-3.
Major Providers—ACH

- **The Clearing House** owns EPN, the other large-scale ACH operator.

- **Local payments associations**—formerly local automated clearing houses—often operate on a regional basis; they serve as their DFIs' connection to NACHA, and also as a source of industry education.

- **ACH processing software vendors and service providers**. All of the large bank "core processors" provide ACH receipt and origination service for their clients.

- The **large originating banks**, which invest heavily in ACH capabilities in order to support corporate origination of transactions. NACHA publishes transaction volumes of ODFIs on an annual basis.

- **Large originators** make their voices heard through their ODFIs and directly to NACHA through a series of councils run by NACHA. Though the councils do not have rule-making powers, both banks and non-banks can participate, and councils have representatives on the NACHA board. The AFP (Association of Finance Professionals), representing enterprise financial requirements, also provides a forum for enterprise input on ACH issues.

- **The U.S. government** is an active user and supporter of the ACH system, and follows the NACHA operating rules.

Summary: ACH

Key Trends in ACH

The simplicity, broad reach, and economic efficiency of the ACH system makes it one of the most important electronic transfer systems in the country. The unique capability of the ACH system to carry large amounts of data along with a payment transaction is enabling interesting new applications, particularly in bill payment and B2B transactions. The ACH system will, however, face continuing competition with better-branded card payments systems that enable different economic models for their providers.

- Growth and complexity: overall, ACH volumes continue to grow and transaction types proliferate. Banks are increasing investment to manage the complexity.

- New ACH transaction types are enabling new forms of commerce and payment, but also increasing risk.

- ACH has been a behind-the-scenes enabler for "alternative payments" providers in the online space. Now ACH is poised to play the same role at the point of sale and for mobile payments.

- International ACH volumes are increasing, and new compliance requirements are focusing attention on these transactions.

- A "same-day ACH" initiative at the Fed may cause the overall processing and settlement environment of ACH to change.

Sources of Information—ACH

- NACHA

- Regional ACH payments associations

- Federal Reserve Bank Payments Services

- *Payments News*

Core Systems: Cards

Overview—Cards	
Type	"Pull payments" with an authorization message
Ownership	Private network ownership
Regulation	Network rules; U.S. law and Federal Reserve Bank regulation
Network Economics	Interchange (merchants to issuers), assessments (issuers and acquirers to network)
Processing	Electronic
Risk Management	Defined by card networks and augmented by processors and end parties

Table 5-1.
Cards Overview

The card payments systems fascinate many people, within financial services and in other industries. They are at the heart of consumer commerce—facilitating trillions of dollars of consumer and business spending each year.

The card systems are compelling because of their sheer size, the extent of their global reach, the staggering degree of standardization and interoperability (enabling a cardholder from Topeka, Kansas to walk into a bar in Singapore and buy a drink, no questions asked), and, perhaps most significantly, the immense profits that have flowed, in particular, to credit card issuers but also to other participants in the payment card value chain.

History and Background

The payment cards industry has its roots in the private department store and oil company "credit cards" issued during the first half of the 20th century. Later, the charge cards issued by Diners Club and American Express in the 1950s, primarily intended for business travel and entertainment (T&E) purposes, established the early "closed loop" card systems.

The card industry as we know it today, however, began in 1966, when Bank of America formed a company, BankAmerica Service Corporation, to franchise its BankAmericard to other banks. Bank of America had launched

BankAmericard in the late 1950s, planning to roll it out across California; in the mid-1960s it began licensing BankAmericard to other banks located outside of California and in a handful of other countries. By 1970, the franchisees began pressing for a new organizational structure for the product, leading to the formation of National BankAmericard Inc. (NBI) to manage the U.S. card program. In the mid-70s, a similar organization was formed to manage the international card program. Shortly thereafter, the two organizations came together under a new company named Visa—with the international organization (IBANCO) becoming Visa International and NBI becoming Visa U.S.A., a group member of Visa International.

Separately, and in competition with Bank of America's card program, another group of California banks formed a competing organization called the Interbank Card Association. The IBA created Master Charge: The Interbank Card and, in 1979, renamed itself and its products to MasterCard.

The early work done by these new companies, structured as associations of member financial institutions, was nothing short of remarkable. They established the principles of open financial institution membership—the open loop exchange of transactions, interchange fees, and brand control through association bylaws and operating rules that would, over time, grow to define the card payments systems. Significantly, these rules set the groundwork for interoperability that quickly grew global, as card systems were developed in other countries and linked into the Visa and MasterCard systems. Interoperability was primarily technical, of course, establishing protocols and timelines for all aspects of issuance, acceptance, and transaction management, but also defined the system economics, brand management, and requirements for transaction interchange. The associations also established arbitration processes for the resolution of disputes between members—ensuring that any such disputes would be resolved "within the family," with association staff acting as court and jury.

Membership

Membership in the open loop associations was strictly limited to banks and other regulated depository financial institutions. Global and regional associations defined their own criteria for admission, related to capital adequacy—a member bank must be able to meet its funding liabilities to the network, and hence to other members. In many countries, the associations relied on existing bank regulatory and supervision infrastructures to handle this task. In the association bylaws, each board of directors set membership voting rights, seeking to balance the needs of small and large participants and giving some "early owner" benefits to founding members.

In joining the card associations, member banks surrendered considerable individual control over how these products worked—but gained the significant benefits of common product definitions and a global acceptance framework that no one bank could develop on its own. Ultimately, some large banks found it frustrating to see the card association brands become stronger and more visible to consumers than the bank's own brand.

Why did banks agree to participate in these associations? The answer is almost entirely economic. The open loop networks, in their early credit-card days, enabled an enormously profitable consumer lending business for card-issuing banks. Originally a means for allowing banks to efficiently, and profitably, lend to their own customers, the credit card quickly opened up, for imaginative banks, a new way to extend lending to consumers outside of an existing geographic footprint. New and profitable customer relationships could be established—on the basis not of a consumer opening a checking account but, rather, applying for a credit card from the bank.

These economics also explain the relative power of card issuing vs. card acquiring banks within the card networks. Although originally many banks were both issuers and acquirers, card acquiring was not as profitable as card issuing. The different economic models of these two sides of the card business led many banks to separate management of card issuing and acquiring, with many banks dropping out of the card acquiring business in the 1980s, after the acceptance environment evolved from paper-based to electronic POS terminals. On the critical operating committees and boards of the card associations, the voice of card issuers dominated the discussion, a situation that continues even within the new ownership structure of the open loop networks.

ATM and Debit Network Formation

In the late 1960s, banks began to introduce ATMs as a new channel for serving checking account customers. The banks issued cards with which customers could access the ATMs, and individual PINs (personal identification numbers) to authenticate the cardholder at the ATM—an unattended card acceptance location with no clerk to compare physical signatures on card and receipt.

Shortly thereafter, retail bank organizations within major banks began forming shared networks to interconnect ATMs and banks within cities and regions. Although similar in some respects to the credit card open loop associations, the shared ATM networks had entirely different economic frameworks—their members were much more motivated by cost reduction (i.e., branch teller expense) than by profit. After all, ATMs weren't lending tools—they simply provided more convenient customer access to cash and reduced the labor associated with accepting deposits.

In the late 1980s and 1990s, the shared ATM networks went through a series of mergers, with a handful of large national networks emerging; Interlink, STAR, and NYCE were the largest. A number of smaller regional networks continue to exist, most operating on an association, nonprofit basis.

Double Innovation?

It is interesting to note that at about the time the ATM networks were being formed, the same departments within the same banks had people working on the fledgling ACH network. At the time, the new networks were responding to very different needs: cash dispensing vs. check replacement. Now, however, the two "grown-up" networks compete for many types of transactions.

By and large, U.S. credit card associations were not involved in these early ATM networks. However, Visa in particular was watching their development—particularly when they began extending acceptance of bank-issued ATM cards to new merchant locations (especially supermarkets and fuel retailers). Banks were interested in having their ATM cards accepted instead of checks, which cost much more to handle and process.

Similarly, merchants appreciated the elimination of checks and their associated bounce risk, while enjoying the benefits of receiving a guaranteed payment when an ATM card was used. The shared ATM networks priced merchant acceptance attractively as an incentive—creating a win-win for merchants, consumers, and banks. But merchants did need to deploy new acceptance equipment—not just to read the card's magnetic stripe, but also to securely accept the cardholder's PIN.

In parallel, credit card acceptance was transitioning from paper-based to a fully authorized electronic environment—and these two systems for merchant acceptance began colliding. This led to Visa and MasterCard developing debit products that would ride over their networks rather than over the shared ATM/PIN debit networks. Along the way, Visa decided to bid on providing processing services to the West Coast-based Interlink network, and did so for many years before ultimately acquiring that network from its member banks. In the process, Visa acquired an ATM/PIN debit network to complement its existing credit card network.

Visa Debit Strategy

Visa believed that debit cards were going to become increasingly important for merchant acceptance. Unsure of how the debit card market might evolve, Visa hedged its bets—by providing processing services and ultimately acquiring Interlink, by becoming an ACH operator (briefly), and by enhancing its credit card network to better meet the needs of consumers and banks for debit products.

Later, in the early 1990s, both Visa and MasterCard introduced their own debit card products, as alternatives to the shared ATM/PIN debit network cards for handling debit transactions. The differences between these two types of cards will be discussed in more detail later in this chapter.

Going Public

Today, the U.S. open loop card networks are no longer owned by banks, but are rather publicly traded concerns—a fact that would have astonished a 1980s card banker.

The first networks to transition to non-bank ownership were the large, shared ATM/PIN debit networks bought by payment processors. In 2004, First Data Corporation bought STAR (through its acquisition of Concord EFS) and Metavante bought NYCE (ironically from First Data, which was required by regulators to sell NYCE after its acquisition of Concord EFS). Banks' willingness to give up control of these networks was largely a matter of cost. The payment processors saw opportunities to participate in increased transaction volumes as debit acceptance continued to expand. As mentioned earlier, the other major shared ATM/PIN debit network, Interlink, had already been acquired by Visa.

Perhaps the most dramatic change occurred in May 2006 with MasterCard's very successful initial public offering of its stock. Later that year, Visa (excepting Visa Europe) announced that it would also go public—and followed with the largest IPO in U.S. history in March 2008.

> **Card Lessons—Debit is Different!**
>
> When Visa and MasterCard executives went to their member banks to discuss the new debit card products, they quickly learned that they were talking to the wrong people! In most large banks, the powerful managers of the credit card issuing businesses had little to do with the people who ran the branch banking network—the retail bank—and who controlled the ATM and PIN debit networks. Full of plans to roll out PIN debit cards, these retail bank executives were not pleased to hear that their plans for the expansion of merchant acceptance were being hijacked by the much more profitable credit card issuing business unit—their rival within the bank. It took a number of years for banks to sort this out, and to focus on the higher profitability of the Visa and MasterCard products relative to the PIN debit products.

Member bank support of these two public offerings was for very different reasons than with the earlier sales of shared ATM/PIN debit networks to processors. The MasterCard and Visa IPOs certainly allowed banks to recognize the value of their investments in the two associations, which had previously been carried entirely off the balance sheet. But much more significantly, the association restructurings into public companies provided the banks with a new way to deal with potential liabilities related to an increasingly challenging antitrust environment.

With their IPOs behind them, the card companies are in a position to acquire, and potentially expand their roles into, a number of new lines of business.

Stage One	Stage Two	Stage Three	Stage Four
Formation	**Expansion**	**Segmentation**	**Diversification**
1960s–1970s	**1980s**	**1990s**	**2000–2010**
Card associations formed Enabled access to credit at purchase Roles of issuer, acquirer defined Interchange defined and established "Honor all cards" rule established Global infrastructure/ interoperability Paper-based system	Expansion to mass consumer market POS terminals replace paper Growth of new acceptance markets High-volume processing Systematic fraud management Brand competition Early affinity cards Early litigation— association wins	No annual fee Co-branding Signature debit issuance, growth Rewards Product and rate proliferation Commercial and purchasing cards eCommerce EMV defined Securitization Association litigation losses	Shareholder ownership Merchant frustrations with fees Prepaid cards Decoupled debit New form factors— contactless, mobile PCI-DSS Security Tokenization, end-to-end encryption PaaS New federal law, regulations

Table 5-2.
A Short History of Cards

The history of the payment card industry is outlined in Table 5 2. When we look back at this history, with its many changes in a relatively short period of time, a few events stand out as particularly important:

- The move, in the 1980s, away from paper to electronic POS acceptance and authorization of every transaction was a pivotal development for the industry. Before that point, a merchant accepting a card payment created a paper "sales draft" and deposited it, very much like a paper check, at the local bank branch. Authorization was done by voice over the telephone, and floor limits (below which transactions were simply not authorized) were common. The card associations significantly accelerated the shift from paper to electronic acceptance by creating a new, lower "incentive" interchange rate that merchants could benefit from if they installed the new electronic draft capture POS terminals. This approach also marked the beginning of the use of specialized interchange rates (separating paper-based acceptance from electronic POS-based acceptance), which later came to be used by the card associations to tackle specialized vertical acceptance markets.

- Card associations have historically been the subject of litigation and regulatory scrutiny. Their unusual structure—and their practice of setting interchange rates as well as a variety of membership questions—raised many questions concerning possible violations of antitrust or other commercial law. A detailed review of the many legal cases in the card industry is outside of the scope of this book, but it is interesting to note that in the early decades of the card industry, the card associations won essentially all major cases. Beginning in the late 1990s, they began losing several significant cases.

Types and Brands

Types

Payment cards may be categorized by type, primarily based on timing of funding—before, during, or after the transaction.

- **Charge cards** are non-revolving credit cards: the cardholder pays in full, at the end of the monthly statement period, for all charges incurred during that month.

- **Credit cards** provide the cardholder easy access to a revolving, unsecured line of credit. The cardholder has the option of paying the balance off in full at the end of the month, or "revolving" and paying the balance over a period of time based upon terms set by the card issuer.

- **Signature debit cards** (so called because cardholder authentication is based upon signature comparison at the acceptance location) access funds on deposit in the cardholder's checking account at the issuing bank. The debit to the cardholder account occurs either on the day of, or the day after, the transaction. In the U.S., signature debit card transactions are carried over either the Visa or the MasterCard network depending upon the bank issuer's choice of card brand. Visa established an early lead with bank issuers of signature debit cards, and continues to be the market leader for signature debit cards in the U.S.

- **PIN debit cards** (authenticated at the acceptance location by the consumer entering a PIN) also access funds on deposit in the cardholder's checking account at the issuing bank. The debit to the cardholder account occurs either on the day of, or the day after, the transaction. In the U.S., PIN debit card transactions are carried over national, regional, or local PIN debit or ATM networks—with routing based on the bank issuer's choice of network participation and the accepting merchant's choice of network routing.

> **Double Duty:** the same physical card, and the same card number, is typically used for both PIN and signature debit. The difference is simply in which network the transaction is routed through for authorization and later for clearing.

- **Prepaid cards** draw funds from an account, most typically held by the card issuer, that has been prefunded by the cardholder (or someone acting on behalf of the cardholder, such as the purchaser of a gift card). Closed loop prepaid cards are usable only at the merchant that issued the card. Open loop, network-branded prepaid cards are typically signature-based and operate over the Visa or MasterCard networks.

Types of Acceptance Environments

Signature-based cards, both credit and debit, work within two primary acceptance environments:

- **Card-present transactions** occur when a cardholder is physically using his or her card to effect a transaction at some type of terminal—or is presenting the card to a clerk who is entering the transaction. Card-present transactions may be at either attended or non-attended venues (for example, a kiosk or vending machine). Card network rules generally protect the merchant from fraud risk in a card-present environment.

- **Card-not-present (CNP) transactions** occur when the cardholder is making a remote purchase—online, by phone, or even by mail order. Card network rules generally do not protect the merchant from fraud risk in a card-not-present environment.

PIN debit transactions have historically been allowed only in card-present environments: PIN debit network rules have required the entry of a PIN into a secure device. This is now changing, as some PIN networks are allowing card-not-present transactions for bill payment ("PIN-less debit") and certain eCommerce transactions.

Brands

As Table 5-3 shows, most major card brands in the United States support most types of cards. American Express, currently with no debit card offering, is an exception. The major regional PIN debit networks, now owned by payments processors, have also not expanded into credit or charge card offerings.

	Visa	MasterCard	American Express	Discover	PIN Debit Networks (e.g. STAR, NYCE, Accel)
Charge Cards	✓ Purchasing Cards	✓ Purchasing Cards	✓	✓	
Credit Cards	✓	✓	✓	✓	
Signature Debit	✓	✓		✓	
PIN Debit	✓ Interlink	✓ Maestro		✓ Pulse	✓
ATM	✓ Plus	✓ Cirrus	(ATM Sharing Agreements)	✓ Pulse	✓
Prepaid	✓	✓	✓	✓	✓

Table 5-3.
Card Brands

Roles and the Value Chain

The card payments value chain, shown in Figure 5-1, has two main components: issuing and acquiring. In an open loop network, an issuing bank serves the cardholder, and an acquiring bank serves the merchant. The card network sits in the middle and manages the physical interchange of the items, the setting and management of rules, and some forms of risk management.

Open loop card networks connect two separate value chains - the **issuing process** and the **acquiring process** - at the point of sale.

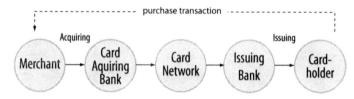

Card processing has a dual message flow: first an authorization message and then a clearing message flow along the same "tracks."

Figure 5-1.
The Card Payments Value Chain

In a closed loop card model, shown in Figure 5-2, the same functions occur, but a single company performs the issuing, acquiring, and network functions. Hybrid models, in which a closed loop network opens up one side of its network to permit other entities to issue and/or acquire on its behalf, are also evolving.

Closed loop card networks perform the same functions as open loop networks—but the issuing and acquiring functions are done by the network itself (or by a processor on its behalf).

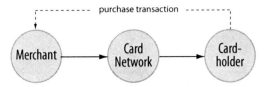

Figure 5-2.
Closed Loop Card Value
Chain

Closed loop networks are more efficient to operate, but may scale more slowly than open loop networks.

Private label cards are a special category of closed loop cards: rather than using a network, these cards are issued by the merchant (or a processor acting on behalf of the merchant), and are usable only at that merchant's outlets.

Card issuance is a term that is easy to understand. The card issuer markets to consumers, receives and validates applications to acquire new customers, furnishes each customer with a card, authorizes and clears card transactions, and provides ongoing statementing, collections, and customer service.

Card acquiring, on the other hand, is one of the least understood parts of the payments industry. At a high level, acquiring is best understood as a set of functions provided to card-accepting merchants, often by different companies, with varying degrees of functional "bundling." In the broadest sense, acquiring refers to functions supporting all of a merchant's needs in card payments acceptance, including POS terminals, software, card processing, dispute management, and merchant customer service. In the narrowest and most formal sense, it refers to the requirement, in an open loop network, that the merchant submit and receive transactions to the network through a contract with a bank that is a member of that network and bound by its operating rules. In practice, the term "acquiring" can include all or only some of these functions.

The functional value chain for debit cards is essentially the same as the value chain for credit or charge cards. Cards are issued, authorized, and cleared over one of the debit networks. The difference between signature debit and PIN debit cards relates primarily to which networks the transactions are processed on, the merchant acceptance environment (PIN-capable or not), and the rules applied by those networks (including interchange).

As Figure 5-3 shows, processors are very important in the card payments systems. Processors handle "on behalf of" functions for both issuers and acquirers. The processing industry is much more concentrated than the banking industry; processors are often more visible, and sometimes more profitable and powerful, than the banks or other third parties for which they process. Processors are more visible on the acquiring side of the business—where they may be the entity a merchant contracts with—than on the issuing side of the business, where they tend to act behind the scenes.

> A processor may perform some or most of the functions of an acquiring or issuing bank. Frequently, physical message switching is conducted entirely among banks, processors, and card networks. On the acquiring side, the processor may be the one entity visible to the merchant, and may be considered to be the "acquirer" by the marketplace. There is always an acquiring bank, however, and this bank bears responsibility to the card network for the transaction.

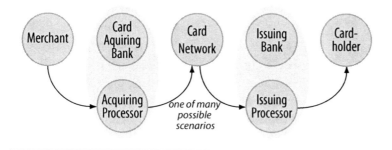

Figure 5-3.
Card Processing

Enabling Technology and Standards

Card networks work because card networks and their member banks have agreed on global standards for physical formatting of cards and definition of key data fields.

The Physical Card

The card itself has defined data fields and locations, both printed or embossed on the physical card and encoded in the magnetic stripe on its back. Although there are variations by card network, region, and country, enough of the data fields are standardized—or commonly recognized—to enable global interoperability of the system.

The key card data element is the PAN, or Primary Account Number. The first six digits of the PAN are the BIN, or Bank Identification Number, which identifies both the card network and the issuing bank. The PAN is both embossed on the card itself and encoded onto two "tracks" of the magnetic stripe.

> **Sponsorship Required**
>
> With open loop networks, the bank itself—either the issuing or the acquiring bank—is always the entity responsible for the transaction to the network. The processor is always sponsored by a member bank in the network. Sometimes, the bank is large and the processor is simply its "hired hand." At other times, the processor is large and visible in the market, and has, in essence, hired the bank to be the sponsor. In either case, however, the technical and financial responsibility is with the bank.

A data element, referred to as CVV (Card Verification Value) or CVC (Card Verification Code), is also encoded on the magnetic stripe, but not physically embossed or printed on the card. It was added to cards in the 1990s to reduce counterfeit card fraud. Earlier, it had been possible to recreate a valid magnetic stripe using just the information on the card (or on a printed receipt). The addition of this data element meant that the card would have to be read in a magnetic stripe reader to capture all data needed to create a counterfeit card.

Another fraud control data element, referred to as CVV2 or CVC2, is the three- or four-digit number printed (in regular ink) on the signature panel on the back (or, for American Express, on the front) of the card, and used for card-not-present transactions. If a merchant captures the CVV2/CVC2 from the cardholder and forwards it in the authorization message to the issuer, the issuer will respond by indicating its validity—or lack thereof. This helps prevent fraud where a card number is known but the physical card isn't present.

There are a number of other features on the physical card, some broadly used and some specific to a card brand, that have been added over time to help reduce fraud.

Chip Cards

In many parts of the world, cards are migrating from magnetic stripe to chip card (smart card) technology. These cards have both magnetic stripes and chips. In markets where the acceptance infrastructure has been upgraded to support chip reading, counterfeit card fraud is much more challenging for fraudsters. However, with most cards usable internationally, including in markets that haven't deployed chip card readers, card fraud may simply migrate out of the domestic environment to other countries—until a universal chip reading infrastructure exists.

Two principle chip standards are used. EMV cards use an industry standard for a "smart" chip (which can handle data encryption). EMV cards are most typically implemented in conjunction with PINs, as in the U.K., which recently adopted the "chip and PIN" standard. EMV-compliant POS terminals read the EMV cards, validate them, prompt the cardholder to provide a PIN, etc.

EMV cards are being introduced on a country-by-country basis as bank issuers and card networks evaluate the costs and benefits associated with their deployment. In the U.S., the common assumption is that the current level of counterfeit card fraud is still too low to merit an industry-wide investment in EMV technology.

Contactless cards use a simpler chip, based on RFID (radio frequency) technology, to pass data between the card and an RFID reader at a POS terminal. Contactless cards are implemented primarily as a customer convenience (for speed of checkout), rather than for fraud management—although they contain technology analogous to the CVV/CVC on the magnetic stripe that helps reduce counterfeit fraud at contactless acceptance locations.

POS Acceptance Terminals

In the United States, a wide range of point-of-sale terminal types can read cards and pass the required transaction data on to the acquirer (either to the acquiring bank itself or the bank's processor). These exist both as freestanding devices and as functionality integrated into ECRs (electronic cash registers) or other devices. The acquirer must route the transaction to the correct payment card network; the network then routes the transaction on to the appropriate issuing bank. Figure 5-4 shows the extensive interconnection of key nodes in the U.S. market's "acceptance grid."

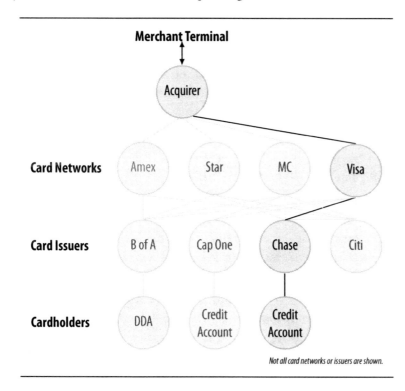

Not all card networks or issuers are shown.

Figure 5-4.
The Acceptance Grid

Card Network Processing

Credit card and signature debit transactions are routed through the acceptance grid twice—once in real time for authorization of the transaction and again (typically at the end of the day) for clearing and settlement.

The card network processing hubs sit in the middle, receiving transactions from acquiring member banks (or, more often, from their processors), sorting and switching them to issuing banks and processors. The card network systems are among the largest online real-time systems in the world and, with extensive redundancy and resiliency built in over the years, hold impressive records for uptime.

The processing environment is quite different, however, for the two message types:

- The **authorization transaction** is in real time, with subsecond response times.

- The **clearing and settlement transaction** occurs in batch, most typically at the end of the day.

PIN debit transactions use a "single message" approach that evolved from their ATM network heritage. ATM transactions never have subsequent adjustments (such as the addition of a tip to a dining purchase), so the single message approach worked well. For PIN debit, the equivalent of an authorization message is sent in real time to the acquirer without a subsequent clearing message. This single message essentially creates its own secondary clearing and settlement message, which is automatically processed—although later and still in batch.

Card Use, Volumes, and Trends

Payment cards are used for many different types of payments. To some extent, these categories define the card products offered by card issuers.

- **General-purpose consumer credit, debit, and prepaid cards** are used for purchases at merchants and other point-of-sale locations, for online purchases of goods and services, and to make bill payments.

- **Consumer cards** are also used for obtaining cash. Debit cards are used for cash withdrawal at ATMs and for "cash back" at certain point-of-sale locations. Credit cards may be used for cash advances at either ATMs or bank branches.

- Businesses use **business credit and charge cards** for travel and entertainment purchases and to make and receive payments from suppliers and customers.

- Both consumers and businesses use cards to make **cross-border payments**; one of the great strengths of the card payments industry has been its ability to conveniently provide this service.

Card Volumes and Growth

Card volume by type looks very different if you look at **transaction count** vs. **transaction amount**. Debit transactions exceed credit transactions by count, but are less by amount due to the higher "average ticket" on credit cards vs. debit cards. Debit cards are increasingly used for "everyday spend"—typically lower-value purchases—while credit cards continue to be used for higher-value purchases, travel, entertainment, etc.

Over the past five years, debit card transaction volume has grown much more rapidly than credit—at the expense of cash, checks, and (to a much lesser extent) credit. Debit card growth reflects the increasing comfort of consumers with using these cards for daily purchasing (replacing checks, cash, and, to some extent, credit cards) and, in recent years, for low-value purchases (replacing cash). Widespread merchant acceptance, particularly for signature debit, makes debit cards easy to use. Some merchants that once accepted checks have also eliminated them from the tender types they support—further fueling debit card usage.

Regulation

Regulations aimed at protecting consumers are controlled by law, as well as in rules promulgated by regulators. The scope of this regulation at the federal level in the U.S. has been increasing as certain payment card industry practices have come under scrutiny in recent years.

Card Network Operating Rules

The operating rules of open loop networks—particularly Visa and MasterCard, and to a lesser extent the PIN debit networks, govern most aspects of card issuing, authorization, clearing, and acquiring. Operating rules are both general (network membership criteria, brand standards, issuance standards, acceptance standards, settlement procedures, arbitration) and specific to card type and type of merchant acceptance (as based on merchant category code). Network operating rules determine the potential profitability of certain card issuing businesses, because those rules specify the card network interchange that applies to a transaction.

Visa and MasterCard rules have historically been very similar. For many years, the common owners of the two associations (formerly, the banks) pressured them for "conformance" of their respective rules. With public card company ownership redefining and sharpening the competition between the networks, an increasing number of rules now differ from one network to another.

In some cases, primarily related either to fraud or to technologies for which standardization is important, the card networks continue to work together. Examples include jointly-owned organizations such as the PCI Standards Council (PCI-DSS data security requirements) and EMVCo (which owns the standards and intellectual property for EMV chip cards).

Card network operating rules may also differ by country and region. Visa and MasterCard have international operating rules that specify treatment of cross-border and interregional transactions. Because cross-border transactions typically involve currency conversion, they produce significantly more revenue on a per-transaction basis for both the card issuers (which typically surcharge them) and the card networks (which handle the currency conversion) than do purely domestic transactions.

Changing existing operating rules for an open loop card network, or creating a new set of rules for a new product, is a complex and time-consuming process. Proposed rules are defined by staff at the card networks and then reviewed with client banks. Depending on the rules, multiple committees may be involved: technical, risk management, marketing, etc. The full economic impact of a proposed rule change may take months or even years to be fully analyzed and understood. Historically, the board of directors of a card network would give final approval for changed or new rules. Under new ownership structures today, final rules approval is done by management. The card networks publish semiannual calendars of upcoming rule changes, giving client banks and their processors time for any system or policy changes needed to implement each new rule.

Network Competition

Keep in mind that card networks compete with each other for payments volume. Rule changes can make it possible for a card network to compete in a new market segment. For example, some PIN debit networks approved rule changes to allow PIN-less debit bill payment. The basic rules of the PIN debit networks require the entry of a PIN into a hardware-encrypted device. This rule effectively shut the PIN debit networks out of the eCommerce domain, and prohibited billers from routing Internet-initiated debit card bill payments through the lower-cost PIN debit networks. The rule change simply removed the PIN entry requirement for certain categories of billers—a segmentation strategy based upon billers not likely to be paid fraudulently. Voilà—the PIN debit networks can now compete for that volume.

Closed loop networks, such as American Express, have card issuance policies similar to some provisions of the open loop card network rules, so as to ensure interoperability for merchants and other users of the payments system. Merchant agreements, for similar reasons, are much like those of open loop card networks. But a closed loop network is free to change such policies and agreements without the involved processes used by open loop networks.

Federal Legislation

The Federal Truth in Lending Act of 1968 resulted in Federal Reserve Bank Regulation Z taking effect the following year. The Act and Regulation Z were aimed at protecting borrowing consumers by requiring full and clear disclosure of terms and rates. Provisions in Regulation Z were strengthened and clarified in 1988 when the Fair Credit and Charge Card Disclosure Act was enacted.

The Electronic Fund Transfer Act, which took effect in 1980, was implemented by Reg E for debit cards. This act was also amended in 2009 to cover gift cards.

In 2009, Congress approved the Credit Card Accountability Responsibility and Disclosure Act of 2009, which significantly increased federal regulation of certain aspects of credit card issuance. Again aimed at consumer protection, the Act specifies detailed requirements on interest rate setting, billing practices, and certain notifications to consumers. The Act stops short of specifying fees or rate caps.

> **Congress in Action**
>
> The 2009 Credit Card Act was most likely inevitable, given the level of consumer outrage over credit card issuers' practices in recent years. Certain issuer strategies such as "double cycle billing" and "universal default" were widely seen by consumers as both unfair and predatory. Consumer advocacy groups kicked into gear and were instrumental in educating legislators, who saw the opportunity to enact legislation popular with consumers. Banks were left with regulation that both constrains their business models and is costly to implement.

Network Economics and Interchange

In the sections that follow, we will discuss the business models for card issuance and card acquiring. But the card companies themselves are also now real businesses, with their own economic models.

The Network Business

Running an open loop card network involves functions such as these:

- Transaction switching among banks participating in the network

- Net settlement among banks, usually on a daily basis and including multi-currency settlement

- Creation, updating, maintenance, and enforcement of operating rules, including setting interchange fees

- Management of network membership, including defining and enforcing criteria (such as financial strength) for membership

- Creation and maintenance of brands and brand promotion strategies

- Arbitration of disputes between network participants

Most networks also provide additional services to network participants. These may include additional processing services, including risk management, and a variety of information products. The rules mandate that participants use some services; others are optional.

The revenue models for the card networks consist of processing fees and brand-use service fees assessed on all transactions made with a card carrying the network brand. The global card networks also earn significant revenue from handling the foreign exchange aspects of all cross-border transactions. Offsetting their revenue are the costs of operating large transaction processing centers; a global telecommunications infrastructure; staff required to handle the rules and perform product management and member relations functions; and the expenses of brand promotion and advertising.

Perhaps the most unusual—and interesting—aspect of the card industry is the networks' role in card interchange. The networks set the interchange rates, but, as we will see, do not directly participate in the interchange financial flow.

Interchange is, however, a critical element of a card network's business model. Since the card network's issuing customers are the recipients of interchange fees, the level of interchange is an important element in the network's competitive position. A higher level of interchange on its card products naturally makes a network's card products more financially attractive to its issuing customers. In a market in which issuers are free to choose among card products from multiple networks, interchange fee income is an important criterion in the decision on which card brand to issue.

Card Network Interchange

Interchange is a feature of open loop card networks. Each transaction involves two banks: interchange is a fee that one bank pays to the other. The network sets the interchange and determines the direction of payment (which bank pays the other). In the United States, interchange flows from the acquiring bank to the issuing bank on purchase transactions; interchange is an expense to the acquiring bank and revenue to the card issuing bank.

The acquiring bank, of course, passes this interchange expense along to its customer, the merchant. The acquiring bank's fee to the merchant is known as the "merchant discount fee," of which interchange is the largest single component. While interchange is often equated with the merchant discount fee, it's not the same thing—just the largest component. This is illustrated in Figure 5-5.

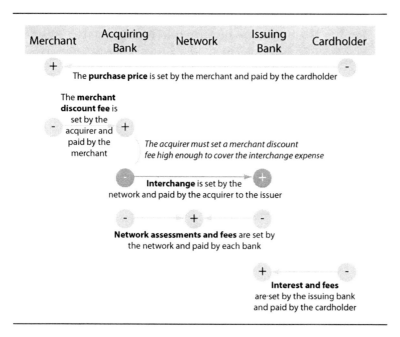

Figure 5-5.
Card Network Interchange

Acquirers typically quote prices to merchants based on "interchange plus" pricing—meaning that interchange fees (along with card network assessments that the acquirers must also pay the networks) are passed through to the merchant with the acquirer's additional fees priced on top of those. With this "interchange plus" approach, acquirers are insulated from changes to interchange fees—they simply pass them through to the merchants, including adjustments the card networks may make to the fees over time. Interchange fees also vary based on the card type used by the consumer and the merchant handling of the transaction; interchange fees are applied, literally, on a transaction-by-transaction level. The rationale for this unusual economic structure rests on the concept that one "side" of the transaction, the merchant (and its acquiring bank), benefits from the use of the card (primarily through increased merchant sales), while the other "side," the card issuer, incurs costs in making this use possible. Interchange is a mechanism to have the value-receiving merchant compensate the cost-incurring issuer for some of the issuer's expenses. It would be too complex, according to this rationale, to have each issuer individually negotiate compensation with each merchant. The network, by defining the appropriate cost reimbursement between the parties, makes the economics work.

The card networks, in the early years of interchange, conducted elaborate third-party examinations of issuers' costs to arrive at an appropriate level of interchange: what one network termed IRF, an "issuer reimbursement fee". The framework used for this examination put costs into three categories:

- **Cost of guarantee.** The card issuer is extending a payment guarantee to the merchant—the merchant is paid even if the cardholder subsequently fails to pay the card issuer what he or she owes.

- **Cost of funds.** The merchant receives payment from the issuing bank (via the card network) before the issuing bank is paid by the cardholder.

- **Operating expenses.** The issuing bank has expenses in operating its authorization network, producing statements, handling customer service, etc.

The Evolution of Interchange

Although each network originally had only one interchange rate, the networks over time realized that setting different rates to accomplish certain objectives was an effective segmentation strategy. The first major incentive rate was introduced in the 1980s, when the networks established a lower interchange rate for transactions handled by electronic draft capture POS terminals in lieu of paper sales drafts. Since then, many additional interchange rates have been defined, for particular merchant categories (for example, a low interchange rate to induce grocery stores to begin accepting credit cards), certain types of transactions (eCommerce, bill payment), and certain types of cards (small business, premium rewards cards, etc.). The interchange rate a merchant pays on a particular transaction is determined by the combination of all such factors. Not surprisingly, given this segmented approach, cost today does not appear to be the sole factor in determining card network interchange.

Interchange rates vary also by payments system. Signature debit card interchange is lower than credit card interchange, and PIN debit interchange is even lower, as illustrated in Table 5-4.

Example - $100 Purchase	Illustrative Rates		
	Interchange	**Acquiring Markup**	**Merchant Discount Fee**
Premium Card Visa Signature MasterCard World American Express*	2.20%	.30	2.50%
Standard Credit Card Visa MasterCard	1.75%	.30	2.05%
PIN Debit Card	.60%	.20	.80%
*American Express does not have interchange, but charges a merchant discount fee equivalent to interchange plus the acquiring markup			

Table 5-4.
Comparative Interchange

Closed loop networks do not have interchange, although the network assesses to the merchant a "merchant discount fee" which is generally similar to the merchant discount fee that an acquiring bank charges for a merchant's access to the open loop networks. In a closed loop network, the entire discount fee is kept by the network rather than being shared among three parties (acquiring bank, network, and issuing bank).

The Interchange Controversy

Interchange has been controversial, in both the United States and other markets. Although the arguments are complex, the two general points of view can be summarized as follows:

Pro-interchange: Interchange is an economic structure necessary to enable a global network of great benefit to all participants; it is the most effective way of managing what economists refer to as a "two-sided market."

Anti-interchange: Interchange is a form of price fixing that unfairly constrains merchants' ability to directly negotiate prices for a key service (card acceptance).

A middle ground holds that the mechanism is effective, but needs some form of governmental control to ensure that interchange rates remain reasonable. This group notes that network competition for issuance leads to rising, rather than falling, prices. This occurs because the network's customer (the issuing bank, which decides which network to use) *receives* the price that the network sets. In a "normal" market, a customer *pays* the price their provider sets.

One concept that has growing appeal among some groups is to not regulate interchange, but instead prohibit card network rules that ban surcharges. This would allow merchants to charge consumers an additional fee for acceptance of high-interchange cards, for example.

In Australia, and to a lesser extent the EU, regulatory authorities have stepped in and mandated reductions in interchange rates. In the U.S., interchange rates have been repeatedly, but unsuccessfully, challenged in court as anticompetitive. Various merchant coalitions have lobbied regulators and legislators in the U.S. for "interchange relief". To the industry's surprise, the 2010 financial reform bill contained a provision—known as the "Durbin Amendment"—that gives the Fed the responsibility to determine appropriate debit card interchange rates. This is widely expected to result in lower debit card interchange. Litigation is also pending in the U.S. with merchants again challenging the legitimacy of interchange fees.

Card Issuance—Credit and Charge Cards

The credit card has been called "the most profitable product in banking history" in the United States. With industry revenues estimated at more than $140 billion annually (accruing to MasterCard and Visa bank issuers, for credit cards alone), it is clearly an attractive business.

In addition to its substantial revenues, three factors characterize the credit card issuance industry in the United States—factors that do not apply in many other countries.

- **Near-universal acceptance.** Almost all retail establishments in the U.S. accept credit cards, as do many non-retail enterprises, including billers, B2B manufacturers, distributors and wholesalers, governments, nonprofits, and educational institutions.

- **A saturated marketplace.** Almost 80% of American households—more than 90 million households or about 175 million individuals—had one or more credit cards at the end of 2008. Many Americans without access to credit have debit or prepaid cards.

- **Multiple cards.** Of Americans who have a credit card, most have more than five cards each. They are used to choosing between those cards at the point of sale based on a wide variety of factors, including available credit lines, rewards, and purpose of the purchase.

These factors have contributed to a sharp increase in the concentration of the marketplace in the United States. The top ten U.S. credit card issuers had over 85% of total general purpose card volume (amount) at the end of 2009.

Table 5-5 shows major U.S. credit card issuers and networks.

Major Providers—Card Issuance	
Issuing Banks	**Co-branded/Private-Label Banks**
Bank of America	HSBC
JPMorgan Chase	Citibank
Citibank	GE Money
Capital One	Barclaycard US
Wells Fargo	**Networks**
U.S. Bank	American Express
	Visa
	Discover
	MasterCard
Not all providers or all categories are listed.	

Table 5-5. Major Providers— Credit Card Issuance

What Credit Card Issuers Do

- **Determine card offerings.** Issuers choose which networks to use, which types of network-branded cards to offer, and which issuer-specific customizations to offer. Major issuers often have hundreds of product variations available. Determining the type and level of rewards offered on a card is an important part of this task. Some baseline card rewards levels are dictated by card network product standards; the issuer customizes others.

- **Solicit new cardholders.** Through mailings, "take-ones," online sites, bank branches, and onsite event leads. Co-branded and affinity cards are a way for some issuers to find new customers at a reasonable cost by partnering with merchants or member associations. Credit underwriting and fraud scoring must be done before approving a new cardholder.

- **Issue cards.** Card issuers must physically issue cards to cardholders, personalized with data on magnetic stripe **and** (for some cards) contactless chips, and manage card activation (preventing fraud from cards lost in the mail).

- **Compete for purchase volume and balances.** Card issuers strive for "top of wallet" positioning—for both POS and online purchases. (Online, a "card on file" at an eCommerce merchant or travel site equals a virtual "top of wallet.")

- **Manage credit and fraud exposures.** The U.S. credit bureaus provide sophisticated tools, which issuers supplement with internal systems, to manage ongoing credit exposure. Other tools, provided by third parties or developed internally, help manage transaction fraud—often dynamically (prior to transaction authorization).

> **What is a Chargeback? (Part 1)**
>
> A chargeback is a card industry term referring to a set of rules that spell out merchant and issuer responsibilities in the event of a disputed transaction. The rules give issuers the right to reverse a credit to the merchant's account (to "charge it back") under certain circumstances based on a series of "chargeback codes" with associated rules and rights. In a very limited set of circumstances, an issuer can charge back a transaction made at the point of sale. But there is also a broad category, known as the "I didn't do it" chargeback, that permits issuers to charge back transactions to card-not-present merchants if the customer claims they did not authorize the transaction.

- **Manage operations, including authorization, clearing, statementing, and customer service.** Part of this is responding to customer and merchant inquiries and disputes—including the so-called "chargeback".

- **Manage the cost of funds.** Issuers also manage the sale of securities to fund additional receivables.

- **Manage collections.** Issuers attempt to collect bad debt from consumers who don't pay off their debts. Issuers often sell bad debt to third-party collectors.

Issuer Support Services

Issuing processors may do some or all of the tasks listed above. A very small bank might entirely outsource its card program so a third party is handling all activity, including taking and managing credit exposure, with the bank simply putting its brand on the product. A larger bank may outsource authorization and clearing, but handle all other tasks in-house; some of the largest issuers perform essentially all functions in-house. Major card issuing providers are listed below. Most of these providers support debit, as well as credit, issuers—and may support prepaid card issuers as well.

Major Providers—Card Issuance Support	
Issuer Processors	**Marketing**
First Data	Acxiom
TSYS	Epsilon
CSC	**Merchant Rewards**
Fiserv	Affinity Solutions
FIS	Mall Networks
Visa DPS	Maritz
MasterCard IPS	Vesdia
Plastics	**Debt Buyers**
CPI Card Group	ASTA Funding
Analytics	Portfolio Recovery Association
Equifax	Encore Financial
Experian	
FICO	
TransUnion	
Not all providers or all categories are listed.	

Table 5-6.
Major Providers—
Credit Issuance Support

Beyond the payment processors, issuers may also rely on other companies to assist in various business areas.

- Specialists assist issuers in using a wide variety of consumer databases to help target potentially profitable consumers for solicitation.

- Issuers may choose to have the actual card plastics produced separately—not by their processor or in house.

- Analytics providers help card issuers with products that assist in predicting credit defaults, adjusting credit lines, and attempting to maximize portfolio profitability.

- Once an account is in collections, issuers may choose to outsource collections to third parties and may, ultimately, sell the debt for a small fraction of its value to a third-party debt buyer that pursues collections independently.

Credit and Charge Card Products

- **Charge cards** have no revolving credit associated with them and require the cardholder to pay the balance in full each month.

- **Revolving credit cards** are the basic credit card we all know so well: the cardholder is given the option to pay the balance in full each month (becoming, in industry parlance, a "transactor") or to make partial payments over a period of time (becoming a "revolver").

- **Premium cards**, in gold and platinum and more, are defined by the card network and offer a variety of special services as well as enhanced rewards.

- **Affinity and co-branded cards.** Affinity cards carry the name and brand of an organization (perhaps a school, alumni association, or football team). Co-branded cards are a joint product offering of the sponsor and the issuing bank. Terms of these deals vary, but generally the sponsor gets some financial benefits (particularly on purchases made at the sponsor's outlets) and the issuer gets a lower-cost source of new customers.

- **Small business cards.** Revolving credit or charge cards offered to small businesses, often with specialized rewards programs.

- **Corporate cards.** Charge cards issued to the employees of a corporation, to be used primarily for travel and entertainment purchases.

- **Purchasing cards.** Charge cards issued to a corporation (to either employees or departments), used to buy goods and services from company suppliers.

- **Private label cards.** Closed loop cards offered by a single sponsor; most common are gasoline and department store cards. Private label cards are not usable at other merchants. Typically, a merchant contracts with a large issuing bank to do the work and take some or all of the credit exposure.

Credit and Charge Card Economics

The economics of the credit card industry are dominated by interest earned on revolving loans to cardholders. The interchange component of the merchant discount fee in an open loop network, and the entire merchant discount fee in a closed loop network, are important but secondary sources of revenue. Charge cards, without the interest income from consumer borrowing, must rely primarily on interchange and cardholder fees for revenue.

Offsetting revenue are credit losses, cost of funds, and operating expenses. The costs of soliciting new cardholders and providing rewards programs both to attract new cardholders and to compete for "top of wallet" position on spending, are also considerable.

The card issuing business is highly profitable. Figure 5-6 shows a typical large credit card issuer's P&L—in "normal" economic times. Note credit losses are shown here as a percent of revenue. More typically, the industry looks at losses as a percent of outstandings. That loss rate is usually around 5%—but in times of recession can climb to 10% or more—resulting in losses for the issuer during those years.

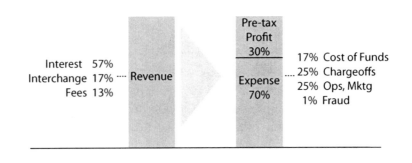

Figure 5-6.
Typical Credit Card Issuer
P&L
Source: Payments Source*,
Glenbrook

Revenue Management

Bank strategies regarding credit vary considerably. Some banks take an aggressive posture, lending to riskier borrowers and compensating with aggressive credit line management and collection policies. Others are more conservative.

Similarly, banks vary in terms of their marketing strategies: some market credit cards only to existing customers who have banking (checking account) relationships with them; others aggressively court new customers anywhere they may live. All banks, of course, are vulnerable to credit cycles in the economy and to how those cycles may affect consumers' ability to repay debt.

Card issuers are becoming more active in their management of credit and charge card interchange revenue. From a credit card issuer's standpoint, the level of interchange income received is based primarily upon the type of card issued. American Express (which now can be issued by other banks), Visa Signature, and MasterCard WorldCard products are higher interchange products, as are small business cards. To increase interchange revenue, issuers have been migrating some existing cards to these products as they go through reissuance, as well as using them for new issuance. The costs of network-mandated rewards programs and other network-defined product features can offset some of the increased interchange revenue.

Rewards Programs

The cost of developing and administering rewards programs is increasingly important to the credit card industry. JPMorgan Chase, one of the top U.S. credit card issuers, reported that in 2008, 58% of its credit card outstanding balances came from rewards cards, compared to 31% in 2003.

Annual card fees, once a common feature of the card industry, have significantly declined in importance; competition has essentially eliminated them for traditional credit cards. But punitive fees for over-limit or late payments, are becoming a more important element of issuer revenue.

*Printed with permission from PaymentsSource.com

Card Issuance—Debit Cards

A debit card enables a customer to make a purchase by using funds from the balance available in a checking account. As shown below, a debit card can be thought of as a hybrid of a credit card and a check; it has similarities to both.

Attribute	Credit Card	Debit Card	Check
Type	Electronic, pull	Electronic, pull	Paper, pull
Source of Funds	Credit	Bank checking account	Bank checking account
Risk to Merchant	Guaranteed	Guaranteed	Not guaranteed
Economics for Issuing (Consumer) Bank	Loan interest, interchange, fees	Net interest income, interchange, fees	Net interest income, fees

Table 5-7.
Debit Card Comparisons

Signature and PIN Debit

In the U.S., there are two primary types of debit transactions: signature debit, routed through the Visa or MasterCard networks ("riding the credit card rails") and PIN debit, routed through one or more of the ATM or PIN debit networks. The physical debit card used for either of these transactions is the same, with the same PAN (primary account number) used regardless of the transaction routing. As mentioned earlier, the evolution of the credit card networks paralleled the evolution of the debit card networks; eventually they came together when Visa and MasterCard launched their debit card products.

The routing of the transaction, however, has meaningful differences in terms of the rules and interchange fees that apply to it.

The routing decision is actually made by a combination of consumer choice and merchant choice at the point of acceptance, and depends on several factors:

- If the merchant does not have a PIN pad, the transaction is always routed through the signature networks. The PIN debit networks require PIN entry at the physical point of sale.

- If the merchant does have a PIN pad, the merchant's system may look up the PAN (using information provided by the merchant's acquirer) and determine that the card transaction can be routed to a PIN debit network. If so, the merchant POS in real time may prompt the consumer for PIN entry, thereby "steering" the transaction through the lower-cost PIN networks, unless the consumer is aware of the difference and asks that the transaction be routed through the "credit" networks (by cancelling the request for PIN at the POS).

- Some merchants do not steer, but leave the choice up to the consumer.

- In card-not-present transactions, routing is almost always classified as signature debit. However, in recent years, the PIN debit networks have been allowing some low-risk transactions, such as online bill payment, to flow through their networks without a PIN—the so-called "PINless debit" acceptance category. Several start-up companies are also attempting to bring PIN debit transactions to eCommerce merchants.

As shown in Table 5-8, the differences between signature and PIN debit are not great. As overall debit purchases continue to grow significantly, bank issuer focus appears to be switching away from a "war between PIN and signature" and simply to more support for debit in general.

Attribute	Signature Debit	PIN Debit
Type	Pull payment	Pull payment
Authentication	Signature	PIN
Merchant Guaranty	Full (Card-present)	Full (Card-present)
Processing	Dual message	Single message
Network Interchange	Below credit card	Below signature debit

Debit Volumes

In the past ten years, debit card volumes have grown rapidly in the U.S. market; they now account for more consumer purchase transactions, on an annual basis, than either credit cards or checks. Recently, the dollar amount of debit card transactions also surpassed that of credit card transactions.

Debit card growth has come as debit transactions have replaced:

- **Checks.** Consumers find debit cards more convenient than checks at the point of sale.

- **Credit cards.** Some "convenience" users of credit cards, who routinely pay off their monthly balance, have switched to debit cards. Others continue to use credit cards, usually to get rewards.

- **Cash.** A more recent trend has been the use of debit cards for very small transactions—particularly now that, at many merchants, a signature is not required for such transactions.

Debit Card Economics

For the consumer's bank, the debit card is not a product in the same sense that a credit card is. A debit card is a component—now, a very important component—of the checking account product. This is true both for consumer and small business checking accounts.

Although some revenues, and some expenses, can be attributed directly to the debit card, the consumer does not make a buying decision to acquire a debit card. Rather, the consumer chooses a bank for his or her checking account, and is then automatically issued a debit card (which, of course, is also an ATM card).

A retail bank P&L might look something like the example shown in Table 5-9: Debit Card Issuer P&L. Note that there is little direct relationship between sources of revenue and categories of expense.

Source of Revenue	Category of Expense
Net interest income: the value of balances in the checking account	Branches, customer service centers
Interchange from purchase card transactions	Systems: transaction processing, networks, statements
Fees: primarily overdraft	Risk management
	Rewards programs

Table 5-9.
Debit Card Issuer P&L

It is clear, however, that increasing the use of debit cards, particularly as they displace check and cash transactions, will grow revenue at a bank. This is simply because the bank earns interchange revenue on every debit card transaction, but nothing on cash or checks. Banks therefore spend time and attention on debit card activation, the industry term used for getting a consumer to start using the debit card—not just for ATM access but also for everyday purchases.

Bouncing Cards

In the early days of debit cards, many banks were wary that debit cards might reduce the NSF ("bounced check") fees from the checking business. Since a debit card was authorized and therefore couldn't bounce, the thinking went, banks stood to lose a lot of the money they were then earning from bounced check fees. After a few years, some smart bankers figured out that they could actually go ahead and authorize debit transactions against insufficient balances, and charge the cardholder an overdraft fee, thereby replicating the NSF income stream. This was so successful that banks increased both the rate and frequency of these charges. This led to a significant consumer backlash against the "$35 overdraft fee on a $5 cup of coffee," leading the Federal Reserve Bank to impose new regulations requiring banks to have consumers "opt in" for overdraft protection.

What the Debit Card Issuer Does

- Issue cards to cardholders, personalized with data on magnetic stripe and (for some cards) contactless chips; manage card activation.

- Choose and manage the ATM and debit card networks, managing the expense of network fees against the interchange revenue (for debit cards) and revenue or expense (for ATMs) offered by the network.

- Manage fraud.

KYC

In order to open a checking account for a customer and issue a debit card, a bank must go through a mandated "Know Your Customer" process. Though this is not generally thought of as a debit card function, a bank can't issue a debit card if it hasn't done this process.

- Manage overdraft and collections on overdrafts extended.

- Manage operations, including authorization and clearing. Note that many operational tasks, including statement production and customer service, are done for the checking account product as a whole, and not specifically for debit cards.

> **Checking Debit Transactions**
>
> Debit card authorization is more challenging than credit card authorization, as the bank must check against an ever-changing account balance. In the early days of debit, banks would authorize transactions (or have a processor authorize them) against a "shadow file" that could be hours or even days out of date. Now, however, most large banks handle authorizations dynamically against the "real" balance in the checking account.

- Define and manage debit card rewards programs. Generally, debit card rewards are less "rich" than credit card rewards, because of the lesser interchange revenue from debit card transactions, which funds the costs of rewards.

Debit Card Competition

Banks' share of the debit card market naturally tracks the distribution of checking accounts. As the U.S. is not a concentrated retail banking market, debit card issuers are much less concentrated than credit card issuers. Also, a consumer may have multiple credit cards, but typically only one debit card. In general, debit card issuance follows a retail bank's checking account market share.

There is, however, competition in the debit brand and network areas—and it is a bit more complex than that for credit cards. Competition exists between the signature debit and PIN debit networks (discussed above), and among brands within signature and PIN debit. Visa and MasterCard compete for signature debit volume, but also own PIN debit networks (in the case of Visa, one of the major ones). There are multiple PIN debit networks, many operating on a local or regional basis. The national PIN debit networks (STAR, NYCE, and Accel/Exchange) are owned by major bank processors.

Major Providers—Debit Card Issuance	
Issuing Banks	**PIN Debit Networks**
Bank of America	STAR (First Data0
JPMorganChase	NYCE
Wells Fargo	Accel (FiServ)
All other banks and credit unions	Interlink (Visa)
Signature Debit Networks	Maestro (MasterCard)
Visa	Pulse (Discover)
MasterCard	Shazam
Not all providers or all categories are shown	

Table 5-10. Major Providers— Debit Card Issuance

Debit Card Rewards

Banks increasingly provide consumers with rewards for debit card usage. This makes sense for the banks, which want consumers to "activate"—and consumers certainly have grown to expect card rewards.

The problem is financial: there isn't a lot of interchange revenue on debit cards to fund the cost of providing rewards. So consumers, used to high reward levels with credit cards, are often disappointed with the relatively low levels of rewards on debit cards. Banks are using a variety of strategies to create rewards programs that satisfy both their desire for debit card activation and consumer expectations:

- **Relationship rewards.** These programs provide consumers with rewards points for a variety of checking account actions; there may be different points awarded for PIN and signature debit, for using the bank's electronic bill payment service, for receipt of an electronic statement, etc.

- **Merchant-funded rewards.** These programs provide richer rewards when a customer shops at one of a set of merchants in the bank's rewards network. The rewards are funded by the merchants. Typically, these networks are "category-exclusive"—they have only one merchant per category (e.g., hardware store or coffee shop).

> ### The Dual Issuance Advantage
> When the card networks introduced signature debit to banks, they didn't permit dual issuance of debit cards—meaning that a bank that issued a Visa signature debit card could not also issue a MasterCard signature debit card. Helped by this policy, Visa took an early lead in debit brand share. Visa's strategy of providing complete debit card processing (card issuance, authorization, and clearing) for banks also helped win bank issuance decisions.

- **Non-traditional structures.** Bank of America introduced "Keep the Change," a rewards program that rounds debit card purchase transactions up to the nearest dollar, then posts the rounded-up amount to the consumer's savings account. The bank then "matches" a small portion of the savings deposit.

New Types of Debit Cards

Although most debit cards in the U.S. use either the signature or PIN debit networks to access funds in a consumer's account, it is possible to use the ACH network to accomplish nearly the same thing. A bank (or a non-bank service provider) can provide a consumer with a card (or a non-card token) that, when presented and authenticated, triggers an ACH debit transaction and pulls funds for the purchase from the consumer's checking account.

Several variations of this setup exist in the market. Although none is large, it is an emerging—and growing area.

- So-called **decoupled debit cards** are "normal" signature debit cards, issued to a consumer by a bank different from the one at which the consumer has a checking account. The issuer authorizes the merchant transaction normally, then uses ACH to pull funds from the consumer's checking account—which the consumer registered upon enrollment. The issuer keeps the signature debit interchange, but bears the risk of NSF or fraud on the ACH transaction. (See also Figure 4-5: Decoupled Debit.)

- Some department stores or gas companies offer **private label ACH cards**. A single-purpose card is given to the consumer, who presents it at purchase; an ACH transaction is triggered. The merchant saves by paying no merchant discount fee, but bears NSF risk. Some grocery stores are "payment-enabling" their loyalty cards in this fashion.

- **Third-party ACH cards** usable at multiple accepting merchants. The third-party provider may take on some or all of the NSF risk. (In the eCommerce domain, PayPal manages ACH debits to consumer checking accounts in this way.)

Card Issuance—Prepaid Cards

Prepaid cards are a special type of debit card. Purchases made with a prepaid card draw on funds already in an account—not upon a line of credit. But rather than drawing on funds kept in the cardholder's checking account, a prepaid card draws on a different type of account, kept on behalf of the cardholder by the sponsor of the card.

There are two types of prepaid cards: closed loop and open loop cards. Closed loop cards are usable only at the sponsor's store or stores. Open loop cards carry a network brand and are usable anywhere that network's brand is accepted.

In the U.S. market, closed loop cards account for roughly three quarters of the prepaid card "load" (value) each year, but the open loop network-branded cards are growing much more quickly. Each type has its own value chain and economic model.

Closed Loop Cards

Most closed loop cards are gift cards. The sponsor of the card is a merchant, which is trying to drive increased sales.

Figure 5-7 shows the basic roles in the closed loop value chain. Roles other than sponsor and bank are optional: a merchant can handle program management and processing in house, and may choose not to use a distributor to have cards sold in other locations.

Gift card programs are often tied into merchant loyalty programs; specialized program managers and processors have designed increasingly intricate product offerings to meet the needs of their sponsor customers. Often, one company provides both program management and processing capabilities.

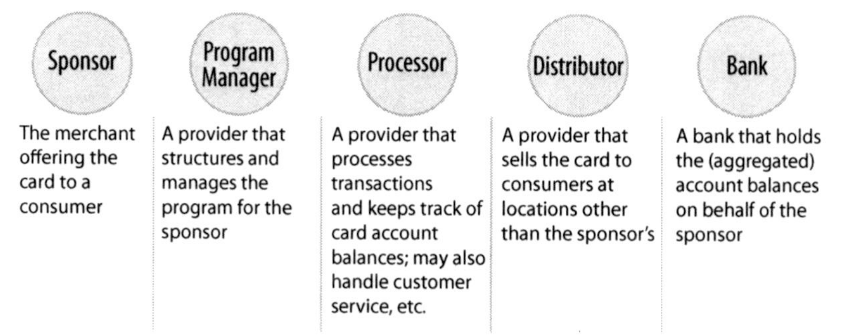

Sponsor	Program Manager	Processor	Distributor	Bank
The merchant offering the card to a consumer	A provider that structures and manages the program for the sponsor	A provider that processes transactions and keeps track of card account balances; may also handle customer service, etc.	A provider that sells the card to consumers at locations other than the sponsor's	A bank that holds the (aggregated) account balances on behalf of the sponsor

Figure 5-7.
Roles in Closed Loop Prepaid Cards

Gift cards are almost always sold to the consumer at face value. The merchant is looking for increased sales, and considers the expenses paid to others in the value chain a reasonable investment. Some merchants, for example, know that they will benefit each time a gift card recipient makes a purchase larger than the gift card amount.

In the early days, some gift card sponsors attempted to charge "inactivity fees" (decreasing the card balance each month), or assigned expiration dates to the card balance. These practices are becoming much less common, however, as they have provoked consumer outrage and regulatory attention.

The role of distributor is an unusual one in payments systems, but highly successful for both the distributor and the distributor's outlets (which sell the cards). Prepaid card distributors emerged as supermarkets and convenience stores figured out that they could profit from selling merchant-branded gift cards at their locations. Consumers expected to be able to choose from a wide range of gift cards at so-called "gift card malls" in supermarkets.

Open Loop Cards

Open loop, or network-branded, prepaid cards are usable wherever that card network brand is accepted—including for purchases, bill payments, and withdrawals of cash at an ATM.

There are dozens of different variations and purposes for open loop cards. Much of today's innovation in the payment card industry is taking place with open loop cards.

Segments of this market include:

- **Business-to-consumer**—rebates, refunds, promotions, insurance claims

- **Government-to-consumer**—benefits, social security, veterans' compensation

- **Employer-to-employee**—payroll cards, incentive cards, bonus cards

- **Consumer-to-merchant**—open loop gift cards, travel cards, youth cards

- **Checking account replacement**—as an alternative to a traditional bank checking account

As shown in Figure 5-8, the value chain and roles are similar to those of closed loop cards, with the important distinction of the network connection.

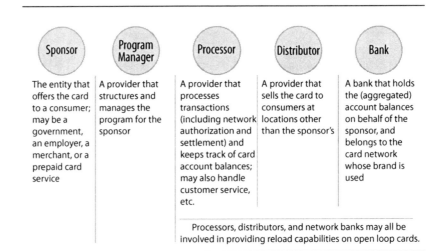

Sponsor	Program Manager	Processor	Distributor	Bank
The entity that offers the card to a consumer; may be a government, an employer, a merchant, or a prepaid card service	A provider that structures and manages the program for the sponsor	A provider that processes transactions (including network authorization and settlement) and keeps track of card account balances; may also handle customer service, etc.	A provider that sells the card to consumers at locations other than the sponsor's	A bank that holds the (aggregated) account balances on behalf of the sponsor, and belongs to the card network whose brand is used

Processors, distributors, and network banks may all be involved in providing reload capabilities on open loop cards.

Figure 5-8.
Roles in Open Loop
Prepaid Cards

Unlike closed loop prepaid cards, the primary motivation is not captive merchant sales at the sponsor's stores. Instead, open loop prepaid cards are designed to make money for the sponsor—the open loop card is sold to the consumer with a premium fee on top of the face value of the card, and a long list of additional fees (monthly maintenance, transaction charges, reload charges, etc.) are common. The prepaid card issuer also receives network interchange on purchase transactions.

A Bank on a Card?

Open loop prepaid cards have been called "a bank on a card," and prepaid card providers have enhanced the capabilities of cards beyond simple purchases and ATM withdrawals. Often, these cards can accept direct deposit of payroll; can be used for online bill payment; and, increasingly, can be tied to savings accounts and/or limited lines of credit. Some highly specialized open loop cards, such as healthcare cards, are good at any network merchant, but only for specific categories of spending approved by the sponsor.

Prepaid Card Regulation

Because of the newness and growth of prepaid cards, the regulatory environment is both uncertain and changing rapidly.

Closed loop cards have been subject to a variety of state laws and, with passage of the Credit Card Act of 2009, new federal regulations. The Act sets new minimum thresholds for fees and expiration dates, but doesn't prevent state laws from being even more restrictive.

Open loop cards are also subject to regulation, including KYC (know your customer) requirements on the card issuer. Open loop cards are also subject to Federal Reserve Board Regulation E. Regulators continue to keep a close eye on these cards to prevent their use in money laundering schemes.

Major providers of prepaid cards are listed below.

Sponsors & Networks	Processors
Wal-Mart	Comdata
Green Dot	FSV
NetSpend	I2c
H&R Block	Springbok
American Express	TxVia
Visa	Vesta
MasterCard	First Data
Banks	TSYS
MetaBank	**Distributors**
The Bankcorp Bank	Blackhawk Network (Safeway)
Palm Desert National Bank	InComm
Not all providers or all categories are listed.	

Table 5-11.
Major Providers—
Prepaid Cards

Card Acquiring

The card acquiring side of the industry can be difficult to understand, because of the variations in roles played by stakeholders. Both processing and economic models vary widely, with significant differences occurring by industry vertical and size of merchant. In this section, we describe core functions and major models in the current market.

Who Is an Acquirer?

This term is frequently confusing, in part because there are at least two ways to understand it.

- From a merchant's perspective, the "acquirer" is the entity that sold the merchant a merchant account, and with whom the merchant deals on a day-to-day basis. This may be an acquiring bank, a processor, a gateway, or, perhaps most typically, an ISO (independent sales organization).

- From a card network's perspective, the "acquirer" is the bank that belongs to the card network and has the contractual liability to the network for the actions of its clients in handling payments within that network.

- From a payments industry perspective, the "acquirer" is the bank or processor bundling most of the functions in the value chain, delivered to the merchant either directly or via partnerships or ISO channels.

Figure 5-9 shows the overall acquiring value chain. Core functions within the chain are usually grouped into "Front-End Functions" and "Back-End Functions".

The Card Acquiring Value Chain includes two sets of processes; any provider may perform some or all of these processes.

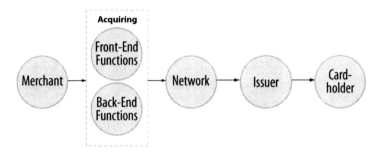

Figure 5-9.
The Card Acquiring Value
Chain

Roles and Functions in Acquiring

The roles described in this section may be performed by many types of companies, in different combinations. The only hard and fast rule is that the acquiring bank must be a network member. Otherwise, it is common to see both big and small providers offering a variety of services—either bundling services for a merchant, or providing one or more services as a part of a bundle that another company has assembled.

Large merchants are more likely to buy acquiring services on an *a-la-carte* basis, assembling the bundles themselves. Smaller merchants are much more likely to buy bundles of fully packaged services. Figure 5-10 depicts elements of the acquiring value chain.

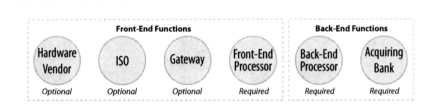

Figure 5-10.
Card Acquiring—
Specific Functions

- **Hardware vendor.** Merchants operating at the physical point of sale need a device to accept the card. This can be either a freestanding POS terminal or a software component in an integrated system such as an electronic cash register. Merchants may buy (new or used) POS terminals or use PCs with card swipe capabilities added. Smart phones may also be used as terminals. Acquirers or their ISOs may supply the necessary hardware and software to merchants. Many industry verticals have specialized systems with integrated payments capabilities; for example, a hotel, restaurant, or doctor's office is likely to use a business management system with integrated payments acceptance capability. In some of these verticals, VARs (value added resellers) play a critical role as authorized distributors of acceptance devices; VARs may also support POS installation and customized software.

- **ISO.** A merchant may buy card acceptance from an ISO, or independent sales organization; an ISO can be a one-person operation or a large organization. The ISO may be "captive"—selling merchant services on behalf of a single acquirer—or may shop for processors and acquiring banks and assemble packages of services for merchants. The ISO business model may be a simple sales commission, or may involve a small share of the discount rate revenue earned from the merchant; in some cases, the ISO takes responsibility for any associated merchant credit risk.

- **Gateway.** A specialized processor that serves the unique needs of a specific merchant vertical group. Gateways may combine the ISO function as well as other value-added services specific to that industry. In the U.S. market, the eCommerce industry vertical is one major user of gateway services. eCommerce gateways played an important role, early in the development of online retailing, by helping online merchants connect to the proprietary formats and systems of acquiring processors. Because of the unique fraud risks borne by merchants for eCommerce payments, these gateways also developed substantial fraud management capabilities. Hotels, restaurants, and airlines are among the other industry verticals that use a variety of gateway services. Gateway fees are typically fixed "cents per transaction" charges.

> **Pounding the Pavement**
>
> ISOs have frequently been referred to as "feet on the street" for acquirers. They have played an essential role in reaching small merchants, in particular, for acceptance of card payments.

- **Front-end processor.** Handles authorization message processing for the merchant. This is a real-time processing business, and again tends to be somewhat specialized by industry vertical. The business model here is also a fixed fee.

The technical interface to most front-end processors uses proprietary formats, making it difficult for merchants to switch processors. Some gateways provide "insulation" by supporting many different front-end processors, thereby allowing a merchant to switch processors more easily without significant system changes.

- **Back-end processor.** Handles the settlement and clearing messages delivered in batch, most typically at the end of a processing day, by the merchant. The back-end processor applies interchange to transactions (including "downgrading" transactions that don't meet the requirements for lower interchange rates) and provides a consolidated financial settlement to the merchant. Chargebacks and disputes come back to the merchant via the back-end processor, and can affect the financial settlement. Reporting to the merchant (help-ing the merchant reconcile actual with expected receipts) is an important part of the back-end processor's function. In addition, the back-end processor most typically generates the bill for acquiring services that it (or the acquirer that has selected it) sends to the merchant. The business model is a fixed fee per transaction with an additional charge for exception items.

- **Acquiring bank.** Every card network transaction must use an acquiring bank. This bank can be the visible "acquirer" in the market or, at the other extreme, a "rent-a-BIN" bank providing card network access to another entity that is the visible "acquirer" in the market. Even in the latter case, the bank is contractually responsible to the network for the merchant's and processor's actions and conformance to network rules. The acquiring bank's revenue model may be a share of the discount fee or a flat fee for use of the BIN.

Acquiring Competition and Market Share

Competition naturally exists within each of the functions listed above. The large players in the acquiring side of the industry often provide all such functions; other businesses may provide only some, outsourcing other elements of the value chain to different processors (sometimes even to competitors).

The Economics of Acquiring

Given the complexities of the multiple providers and bundles involved, we will now take a step back and describe the overall economics of merchant acquiring. The comments in this section apply to the fees paid by a merchant (to one or more providers) and the costs of servicing a merchant (although the service may be performed by one or more providers).

Acquiring revenue is largely based upon the merchant discount fee—the price charged by the acquirer to the merchant. This is normally expressed as a fixed fee plus a percentage of the value of the transaction. Since card interchange fees (charged by the issuer to the acquirer) are such an important component of acquiring expense, the acquirer often prices services to the merchant on an "interchange plus" basis. A merchant discount fee, therefore, may have a price of "interchange plus assessments" (the card network fee assessed to the acquirer) plus "x cents per transaction plus y% of the transaction value."

Other sources of revenue include float (funds received from the card issuer but not yet paid out to the merchant), monthly fees, and exception handling fees.

The expense side of acquiring includes:

Reading the Fine Print
Acquirers' bills to merchants are notoriously complicated and long—a real case of "the devil is in the details."

- Interchange fees

- Card network assessments

- Merchant acquisition costs

- Systems development, maintenance, and compliance

- Processing costs

- Merchant servicing costs

- Credit losses

- Fraud losses

It may seem surprising that the acquiring side of the business is exposed to credit and fraud losses. But the acquirer is responsible to the card network (which is responsible in turn to the issuer) for the good behavior of its merchants. A fraudulent merchant, which as an example ships "empty boxes" or knowingly sells fraudulent goods, will result in cardholder disputes and chargebacks on those transactions back to the merchant. If the merchant has disappeared, or if its account cannot fund the chargebacks, the acquirer bears the financial responsibility. Because of this, fraud management of merchant accounts is an important part of the acquirer's job.

Credit exposure can be even more serious. Certain types of merchants, such as airlines, sell tickets in advance of service delivery. If an airline goes out of business between the time it collected payment and the planned use of the ticket, the cardholder will often, under the card network rules, be able to charge back the transaction for services not received. The financial obligation in this case falls on the acquiring bank. Because of this risk, many acquirers demand hefty guarantees, or hold funds in escrow, for at-risk merchants and merchant categories—or simply choose not to service those merchants/categories because of the potential credit risk.

Major players in card acquiring are listed in Table 5-12: Major Providers - Card Acquiring.

Major Providers—Card Acquiring	
Acquirers	**Gateways**
First Data	CyberSource
Chase Paymentech	PayPal
BA Merchant Services	Retail Decisions
Fifth Third	Merchant Link
Elavon	Merchant Services & Software
Wells Fargo	ACI
Global Payments	ISD
Heartland Financial	
RBS	
POS Terminals & Software	
VeriFone	
Hypercom	
Ingenico	
VIVOtech	
Micros	
NCR	
Not all providers or all categories are listed.	

Table 5-12. Major Providers— Card Acquiring

Card Risk Management

Risk management for credit cards concentrates primarily on credit risk—the risk of the cardholder defaulting on card loan balances—and, to a lesser extent, on fraud risk. On an industry-wide basis, credit card fraud is much smaller, in terms of dollar amount, than credit losses.

Credit Risk

A credit card issuer is obviously taking on credit risk when extending a line of credit to a new cardholder. Issuers control this risk through a credit approval process at the time of account opening, and via periodic reviews of the cardholder's account and behavior.

Credit bureaus are a critical component of the credit risk management process: they provide a comprehensive view of a cardholder's credit exposures and payment behavior with multiple lenders. Credit bureaus and card issuers have become increasingly sophisticated in using—and automating—the tasks of reviewing a cardholder's status and deciding on actions (increasing or decreasing lines, sending an account to collection, etc.). Credit bureaus, issuers, and third parties use scoring techniques to evaluate a cardholder's potential for loan repayment. In recent years, credit bureaus have developed products that can deliver credit scores on potential new cardholders in real-time, thereby enabling "instant issuance" of credit card accounts.

Charge card issuers also take credit risk, but for a shorter time period, as cardholders are expected to repay account balances at the end of each billing period.

Debit card issuers take no credit risk unless they authorize a transaction against insufficient funds, thereby approving an overdraft loan to the consumer. In doing so, they have credit risk exposure similar to that of the charge card issuer—though the consumer is expected to repay the overdraft quickly, usually within the next day.

Fraud Risk

Credit and debit card fraud, and fraud risk management, is a highly developed science—on the part of both fraudsters and the card issuers, acquirers, and merchants that counter fraud. There are a few important concepts to recognize in understanding card fraud:

- Fighting card fraud requires sophisticated analysis techniques—and real data. One of the most important functions played by the card networks in this area is the accumulation of fraud reports coming from issuers (issuers must report fraud when discovered), and the analysis of those reports.

- Card fraud is responsive to efforts to control it, although it mutates. When the industry identifies a fraud technique as significant enough to merit a concentrated attack against that fraud, actions are taken to drive it down. Almost always, however, fraud pops up again with another technique, or a different angle or target.

- Credit card issuers have learned that it works to band together and share resources in fighting fraud. The card networks play a primary role in facilitating those efforts. (Credit risk, on the other hand, is dealt with very much on an issuer-by-issuer basis, and managing credit risk is seen as a key competitive differentiator.)

- For both credit and debit cards, there is a major difference in rules between card-present and card-not-present environments. Card network rules allocate fraud liability to the card issuer in card-present acceptance environments, while the fraud liability in card-not-present acceptance environments is allocated to the card acquirer (and, therefore, is ultimately borne by the card-not-present merchant). If a cardholder claims, "I didn't do it", (that is, I didn't make the purchase that appears on the statement) and the transaction occurred at a physical store, then, when the cardholder's account is credited, the card issuer bears the loss—the merchant keeps the sale. In a similar situation, if the transaction occurs at an online retailer, the card issuer can charge back the transaction to the acquirer—which then debits the merchant's account.

Types of Card Fraud and Fraud Control Mechanisms

- **Lost and stolen fraud.** Someone other than an authorized individual uses a legitimate card account in a card-present environment. The earliest and most basic defense introduced to deal with this type of fraud was signature checking. Recognizing the limitations of this as a control, issuers (or their processors) use sophisticated decisioning tools as part of their authorization systems, to try to detect unusual and suspect transactions. When a cardholder reports a lost or stolen card, the account is closed, authorization denied, and a replacement card sent to the cardholder.

- **Counterfeit.** The card's magnetic stripe data has been duplicated on a new piece of plastic and is used by a fraudster. This very popular fraud was particularly easy to pull off in the early days of credit cards, when a counterfeit card could be created from just the data visible on the card (name, expiration date, account number). In the 1980s, to counter increasing counterfeit fraud, the card networks enhanced the mag stripe with the addition of the CVV/CVC2, a code that does not appear physically on the card itself. As a result, to create a counterfeit, a fraudster must read the mag stripe ("skimming") or intercept a stored image of it. (In recent years, the PCI-DSS standards have imposed a stringent requirement on industry stakeholders preventing storage of any mag stripe data—because of the significant value of stripe data to counterfeiters). Another defense against counterfeit fraud is the authorization decisioning systems mentioned above.

- **Card not received.** A newly issued card stolen en route to the legitimate cardholder and used by a fraudster. This fraud has been successfully countered by requiring cardholders to call the card issuer to authenticate themselves and activate a new account.

- **Identity theft.** A card account has been fraudulently opened in the name of another consumer (real or fictitious). Card issuers rely on a number of shared databases, operated by the card networks and by third parties, to identify potentially fraudulent new account applications. Such a database might highlight, for example, a phone number associated with a previously identified fraudulent account.

- **Identity creation.** A fictitious identity has been created, and a card account opened in the name of the fictitious person. Again, the control against this is the use of shared negative identity databases.

- **Unauthorized use.** A legitimate card account is used by an unauthorized individual in a card-not-present environment (Internet, mail, or telephone order). The risk in this case is borne by the card-accepting merchant, not the card issuer. Merchants use a wide variety of techniques—both internal and third-party services—to identify potentially fraudulent transactions. One popular method is the use of address verification services provided by the card networks. The three-digit CVV2/CVC2 security code that appears on the signature panel of a card is sometimes requested by the merchant to provide some proof of physical possession of the card.

- **"Bust out."** A legitimate card account is used by an individual who has no intent to pay off the balance. This type of fraud is controlled with the same tools used to monitor credit risk exposures.

> ### Security Technologies
>
> The card networks have made multiple attempts at improving the security of card-not-present transactions. In the mid-1990s, the card networks jointly developed a digital certificate-based security system known as SET, or Secure Electronic Transactions. After this failed to be adopted, the networks began to promote what was called internally "3-D Secure" (three-domain secure), which adds a requirement that the consumer enter a password to be verified by the issuer during authorization of an eCommerce transaction. This protocol, branded as Verified by Visa and MasterCard Secure Code, has had some success in other parts of the world, but very limited success in the United States. Critics note that in the U.S., card issuers assure customers that they will have "zero liability" in the case of eCommerce fraud—giving consumers little reason to adopt the protocol and issuers little rationale to promote it.

- **PIN debit fraud.** The rules of the PIN debit networks require hardware-encrypted devices for PIN entry, to verify the consumer. As a result, fraud in card-present environments is limited. When it does occur, it is typically because of theft of both the PIN and the physical card. In one scenario, a fake ATM front accepts and reads the magnetic stripe of a debit card, while a hidden camera records the PIN entry.

Data Security and PCI

The growing sophistication of fraudsters in hacking computer networks and stealing payment card data has created a huge problem for the card payment industry. Processing system intrusions have compromised millions of card accounts simultaneously. In addition to leading to fraudulent card usage, these attacks have been costly for issuers (which must both handle the public relations issues and decide whether to reissue cards on potentially compromised accounts) and detrimental to the industry as a whole (as they reduce consumer confidence in the integrity of the card systems).

But the real weight of addressing the problem has fallen on the shoulders of merchants and their acquirers. Most such attacks have been made on merchant payments acceptance systems, or on merchant acquirers or processors. To combat this problem, the card networks joined forces to form PCI-DSS—the Payment Card Industry Data Security Standard. Known as PCI, it is a set of requirements designed to protect cardholder data on merchant and processor systems. Following agreement on the requirements, to drive compliance the card networks began to require compliance assessment for stakeholders, and to fine violating merchants and processors—sometimes significantly. PCI compliance is an important step, but it is becoming evident that attacks are still possible. Several other initiatives are underway to further protect card data, including tokenization (which substitutes a placeholder number for the actual card number) and end-to-end encryption (to protect card data from being entered into point of sale acceptance locations).

Major providers in card fraud management are listed in Table 5-12.

Risk Scoring	eCommerce Fraud Management
FICO	Accertify
Experian	CyberSource
TransUnion	41st Parameter
Equifax	Verifi
ID Analytics	Kount
Visa/MC—Issuers Clearinghouse	**PCI-DSS**
	Many different assessors
	Multiple tokenization and encryption suppliers

Table 5-13.
Major Providers—
Card Fraud Management

Not all providers or all categories are listed.

Summary: Cards

The card payments systems in the United States have shown dramatic growth, and significant utility to both users and providers of the systems. Card systems are likely to see, however, increasing regulatory oversight, pressure on interchange, and competition from ACH-based products and providers.

Key Trends in Cards

- Continued concentration among credit card issuers
- Continued growth of debit transaction volume at expense of cash and checks
- New regulatory pressures on both credit and debit issuers—providing increased consumer protection
- Ongoing debate, litigation, and regulation about merits and levels of card interchange
- New form factors: chip, contactless, mobile, etc.
- Continued support of rewards programs for both credit and debit

Sources of Information—Cards

- *Payments News*
- The Nilson Report
- Cards&Payments (Source Media)
- Visa, MasterCard, American Express
- Philadelphia Federal Reserve Bank Payments Card Center
- Mercator
- Tower Group
- EFTA

Core Systems: Cash

Overview—Cash	
Type	**Push payments**
Ownership	No ownership
Regulation	U.S. law and Federal Reserve Bank regulation
Network Economics	ATM withdrawals subject to network interchange

Table 6-1.
Cash Overview

Cash is, in many ways, the most simple of the payments systems in the United States. As a self-clearing "push payments" payments system, it has none of the complexities of either open or closed loop systems. It is a virtual payments system—no one owns it, and no one writes "the rules" for cash. Interestingly, it is the only form of payment that can be used anonymously on the part of both payer and payee. Perhaps because of this simplicity, it remains both the most commonly used form of payment and the least understood. In this chapter we will explore how cash gets into the economy, what's involved in its use and circulation, and who profits from the system.

Cash Volumes

No one really knows the true number of cash transactions in the U.S. economy. Reasonable estimates have been made for cash payments at larger stores, and for bill payments. But there obviously is no way to accurately count person-to-person transactions. The same is true for many payments to small or personal businesses, as well as cash payrolls paid to temporary or "off-the-books" employees. In addition, of course, there is significant cash usage within the criminal economy. Finally, some economists estimate that as much as 60% of cash produced in the U.S. is actually held overseas.

> In *Greenback*, his book about cash, Jason Goodwin notes, "There are more dollar bills in existence than any other branded object, including Coke cans."

Cash Production and Supply

Cash is physically produced by the U.S. Treasury's Bureau of Engraving and Printing (notes) and the U.S. Mint (coins). The only way that cash can get physically into the economy is if a bank with an account at a Federal Reserve Bank orders cash. The Fed then debits the bank's account for the amount ordered, and tells the bank to come and collect the cash.

Banks then need to deliver the cash to their vaults at branches, to their ATMs, and to merchants that have put in orders for cash; armored car services supply the trucks and the personnel to do this.

Cash gets into the economy when a Federal Reserve Bank member bank buys cash from the Fed. End Party then receives cash from banks through branches or ATMs.

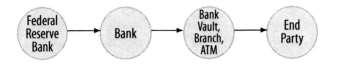

Figure 6-1.
The Cash Value Chain

Cash Acceptance

Merchants that accept cash need to have the personnel and secure storage systems to handle it, as well as procedures and systems to control both employee and customer theft.

The cost of cash acceptance by merchants varies according to the type of merchant and the size of the cash payments. There are few purely variable costs associated with cash: cash handling, depositing, and fraud (theft) control expenses are largely fixed. One result of this is that a merchant who slightly reduces the percentage of cash payments is unlikely to see a corresponding reduction in expense.

Cash Deposit

Consumers and enterprises deposit cash at banks. Banks need to be able to count and securely store the cash. Some banks accept cash deposits at ATMs as well as at branches. Many banks offer late-night deposit vaults for businesses needing to deposit end-of-day proceeds. Banks charge enterprises for frequent or large cash deposit activities. A large cash-accepting merchant will often count, wrap, and bundle cash prior to deposit in order to reduce these fees. Recently, banks have been offering some merchants "on-site vaults": the merchant deposits cash into a secure vault, which (somewhat like an ATM) counts and verifies the cash; the cash is then deemed to have been deposited into the bank, which periodically has the cash picked up by an armored car service.

Grocery stores and other high-frequency, cash accepting merchants "recycle" cash by providing cash back at the point of sale to PIN debit customers.

Banks also routinely screen currency to detect counterfeits (as do some large merchants); most counterfeit currency is caught in this manner.

Banks themselves can deposit excess, worn, or damaged currency at the Federal Reserve Bank; worn or damaged currency is then destroyed.

ATMs and ATM Networks

ATMs are the most common way that U.S. consumers get cash from their bank accounts. ATMs were introduced in the U.S. first in the 1970s, primarily to reduce branch operations expenses, but also to provide convenience to customers.

Today, ATMs are operated by banks, both on their own premises and "off-premises," and by nonbanks. With current ATM network interoperability, a consumer in the U.S. can generally get cash from any ATM. Figure 6-2 depicts the ATM value chain.

A consumer may withdraw cash (1) from his or her own bank; (2) from another bank, which connects to the consumer's bank through an ATM network; or (3) from a nonbank, which connects to the consumer's bank through a relationship with another bank (which, in turn, belongs to an ATM network).

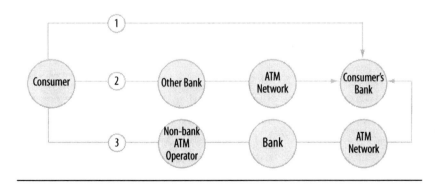

Figure 6-2.
The ATM Value Chain

There is a fairly complex flow of fees connected with the ATM industry.

- A bank may charge a customer for withdrawing cash from its own ATMs, but this is atypical; most often, ATM withdrawals (perhaps up to a monthly limit) are included in the checking account "package."

- If a customer goes to another bank's ATM to withdraw cash, a number of fees may apply:
  - The ATM network that connects the two banks sets an interchange fee, which the customer's bank pays to the bank whose ATM was used. (This can be thought of as "backward interchange," as it flows away from the customer's bank, rather than toward it as for POS debit transactions.)
  - The bank whose ATM is used may assess a fee (the "surcharge"), which is taken out of the customer's account along with the withdrawal.
  - The customer's bank may assess a fee to its own customer for using a foreign ATM; this is intended to offset the interchange that the bank had to pay on that transaction.
- If a customer goes to a non-bank ATM, the fees are similar to those above. The non-bank ATM must contract with an ATM network member bank in order to connect to the customer's bank account. The non-bank ATM owner and the bank it contracts with reach an agreement to share the revenue from the customer (the surcharge) and the revenue from the customer's bank (the interchange).
- One or more of the bank or non-bank ATM owners may contract with a processor to provide network access, or to service its ATMs ("ATM driving"). A facility owner (a store, for example) may also be paid for hosting the ATM.

There are a number of "surcharge-free" ATM networks in the U.S. A bank (or prepaid card issuer) joining one of these networks enables its customer to withdraw cash at a network ATM without being exposed to surcharges by the foreign bank. The foreign bank still receives interchange from the customer's bank.

Cash Regulation and Risk Management

Because of extensive use of cash in the criminal economy, there is a significant amount of regulation around cash deposits. The Bank Secrecy Act of 1970, and later the Patriot Act of 2001, created obligations on the part of banks to report large cash deposits, in order to reduce money laundering. Banks that fail to comply face significant fines.

Counterfeit currency is an ever-evolving fraud problem. Technological advances in imaging and printing have made counterfeiting easier; as a result, banks and processors have installed ever more sophisticated counterfeit detection equipment.

Major Providers

Major industry providers are listed in Table 6-2.

Banks	ATM Manufacturers
Banks	**ATM Manufacturers**
The Federal Reserve	Diebold
Cash Delivery Services	NCR
Loomis	**Non-bank ATMs**
Garda	Cardtronics
Brinks	Payment Alliance
Anti-Money-Laundering Software	**Surcharge-Free Networks**
Oracle/Mantis	Allpoint (Cardtronics)
Actimize/Fortent	MoneyPass
Counterfeit Detection Hardware	
AceDepot	

Not all providers or all categories are listed.

Table 6-2.
Major Providers—
Cash Services

Summary: Cash

The grip of the cash payments system on small-value transactions appears to be finally loosening. The advantages of simplicity, convenience, and anonymity will, however, continue to make it a significant force in the world of payments.

Key Trends in Cash

- Use of cash falling at POS

- On-premise merchant cash vaults as bank deposits

- Envelope-free ATMs leading to increased ATM deposit activity

- Unbanked consumers with open loop prepaid cards driving ATM volumes up

Sources of Information—Cash

- The Federal Reserve Bank Payments Services

- Bureau of Engraving and Printing

- U.S. Mint

- NAAIO (ATM association)

- EFTA

Core Systems: Wire Transfer

Overview—Wire Transfer	
Type	**Push payments**
Ownership	Fedwire: Federal Reserve Bank CHIPs: The Clearing House
Regulation	Federal Reserve Bank regulation and private network rules
Network Economics	Clears at par
Processing	Electronic
Risk Management	Managed by networks, intermediaries, and end parties

Table 7-1.
Wire Transfer Overview

Background

Wire transfer systems carry the serious money in the U.S. Payments Systems. Also known as "large-value systems," the U.S. wire transfer systems, and their counterparts throughout the world, are designed to handle very high-value transactions between businesses, and most often between financial institutions.

Unlike most industrialized countries, the U.S. has two such systems: Fedwire and CHIPs. An important third system, SWIFT, is not a payments system but a global financial services messaging system frequently used in conjunction with the large-value systems.

Most large-value systems worldwide have been modified over the past twenty years to become real-time gross settlement (RTGS) systems. These systems do not use the "net settlement" process typical of all paper and electronic consumer systems, instead settling each transaction individually as it occurs. This gross settlement is necessary to avoid the risks associated with bank failure. With hundreds of

> ### The Legacy of Herstatt Risk
>
> The failure of the German bank Herstatt in 1974, during the course of a day, caused huge losses worldwide and a cascade of bank failures. This type of risk, which became known as "Herstatt risk," led to the development of RTGS and CLS (continuous linked settlement) systems worldwide.

billions and sometimes trillions of dollars transferred daily, a net settlement system would expose the network—and therefore the network owners—to intolerable risks if only one member bank failed during the day.

Volumes

Large-value systems account for a small fraction of total payments systems transactions but a very large percentage of dollar value. In large part, this is because of the financial transactions (such as foreign exchange transactions and securities settlements) that flow through the networks.

Uses and Purposes

Wire transfers are commonly used for:

- **Time-critical payments** such as large-value purchases with specific payment dates.

- **Fully guaranteed payments.** A wire transfer cannot be repudiated, reversed, or charged back without the agreement of the recipient.

- **Immediate payments**, for example, for the sale of a security or the settlement of a trade.

- **Financial institutions**, including banks and securities firms, which routinely use wire transfers for the settlement of financial market transactions. Businesses make some, but not most, of their supplier payments via wire transfer. Consumers rarely use wire transfers, with the exception of transactions such as real estate purchases.

The Value Chain

The sender of funds instructs his or her bank to send a wire transfer to a receiver. The value chain below shows both banks belonging to the same wire transfer network. In other cases, the sender's bank or the receiver's bank (or both) execute the transaction through correspondent relationships with banks that belong to the network.

Figure 7-1.
The Wire Transfer
Value Chain

Fedwire

Fedwire is a service of the Federal Reserve Banks. It is available to banks that have an account at one of the Federal Reserve Banks. (All nationally-chartered banks must have an account at a Federal Reserve Bank, and state-chartered banks have the option of opening such an account.) Fedwire is, in essence, a super-sized online banking service.

The wire transfer value chain (shown in Figure 7-1) is deceptively simple. As an example, an enterprise wanting to send a wire transfer sends an electronic message to its bank. The bank debits the account and sends a message to Fedwire. The Federal Reserve Bank at which the account is domiciled debits the bank's account and credits the account of the receiving bank. The receiving bank then credits the account of the receiving company. All of this is done online, in real time. Of course, the electronic messaging is done with a high degree of security, usually (depending on the type of connection, and bank policy) including encryption and the use of hard-token authentication devices. Many companies also opt to have wire transfers subject to dual internal approvals.

The core management problem for all value chain participants is risk. Before sending the instruction to the Fed, the sending bank must be absolutely sure that there are good funds in its customer's account. Before crediting the receiving bank, the Fed must be absolutely sure that there are good funds in the bank's account. Thousands of transactions and hundreds of millions of dollars flow instantaneously through these systems, and it is critically important to avoid mistakes.

If the sending company does not have sufficient funds in its account, but is expecting incoming funds shortly to cover the transaction, its bank may extend a daylight overdraft. This is a loan; if the incoming funds never materialize, the bank must collect funds from their customer or face a loss. Similarly, the Fed may extend a daylight overdraft loan to the sending bank. Together, the participants in the system watch the flow of funds and in particular try to manage blockages; a failure of one bank to promptly credit its customer's accounts with incoming transfers will result in an inability to process outbound transfers.

CHIPs

CHIPs, or the Clearing House Interbank Payments system, is a private sector alternative to Fedwire. CHIPs is owned by The Clearing House, which in turn is owned by large banks in the United States. It is similar to Fedwire in being a real-time, fully guaranteed system meant to handle high-value payments. Unlike Fedwire, however, which is accessible to any bank with an account at a Federal Reserve Bank, CHIPs is used by only a small number of very large banks. CHIPs is not an RTGS system, using instead a form of multilateral netting that manages settlement risk while providing certain liquidity benefits to participating members.

SWIFT

SWIFT can be thought of as "the payments system that isn't a payments system." SWIFT is a global messaging network for the financial services industry, through which participating members, including banks and securities firms, can send each other secure, structured messages. Many of these messages are payments-related; one might instruct a financial institution to initiate a payments transaction in a wire transfer or other type of payment network. SWIFT has recently opened up its messaging network, allowing corporations to use it to deliver instructions or receive data from participating banks, without the need to maintain separate connections to each bank.

Wire Transfer Regulation and Risk Management

Wire transfer transactions are governed by Article 4A of the Uniform Commercial Code, and by the operating rules of the network (Fedwire or CHIPs).

Risk management, particularly the prevention of fraud, is very important for wire transfer services. Consumer payments systems, both paper and electronic, assume a certain amount of fraud. The cost of these fraud losses is covered by the revenue (fees, interchange, interest, float) earned on good transactions. But this doesn't work with wire transfer systems: there is no price a bank can set on a "good" wire transfer that would cover the bank for the loss, for example, on a single fraudulent $500 million transaction. So participants in the value chain, particularly the banks and network operators, surround the network with a complex (and expensive) web of risk management systems, procedures, and people.

Economics

Wire transfer economics are very different from those of consumer payments systems. The incremental cost of processing transactions is relatively low—the Fed, for example, normally charges a fee of well below a dollar to process a transaction through Fedwire. (The exact cost depends on volume—the Fed publishes its price schedule on its website.) The banks, however, charge their customers—both on the sending and receiving side—fees that can range from $3 to $50, again depending on the bank's relationship with the customer and the volume of transactions processed. The difference between the incremental cost of processing through Fedwire and the price to customers reflects the expense associated with maintaining the risk management systems described above, as well as supporting secure connectivity to the bank.

Major Providers

Major industry providers are listed in Table 7-2.

In addition to the network providers, the wire transfer industry has traditionally been dominated by what have been called the "Money Center Banks"—the New York City-based banks that provided banking services to Wall Street firms. That concept is somewhat dated now but the same banks still lead market share positions in the wire transfer business. Many run significant correspondent banking businesses, and connecting smaller correspondent banks to the wire transfer systems is an important piece of that business.

Banks	Networks
Bank of America	Fedwire
JPMorgan Chase	CHIPs
Citibank	**Software & Services**
Wells Fargo	Fundtech
BNY/Mellon	ACI Worldwide
ABN AMRO	SunGard
Not all providers or all categories are listed.	

Table 7-2.
Major Providers—
Wire Transfer

Summary: Wire Transfer

The wire transfer systems have an unchallenged position in handling financial market transactions. The future may show increased use of wires for commercial, and possibly consumer, transactions.

Key Trends in Wire Transfer

- Wire transfer networks are enhancing their ability to carry remittance data along with payments, in order to further penetrate the B2B supplier payment market.

- More trade is cross-border, and bank wire transfer services are increasingly helping corporate customers manage delivery of cross-border payments to other countries, as well as managing associated foreign exchange transactions.

Sources of Information—Wire Transfer

- The Clearing House—CHIPS

- Federal Reserve Bank Payments Services—Fedwire

- Association for Finance Professionals (AFP)

- SWIFT

- SIA (Securities Industry Association)

Perspectives on Payments Systems Users

Introduction

This chapter begins a two-part look at the stakeholders that participate in any payments system. First, we'll explore the user perspective—looking at what's most important to the senders and receivers of the funds that flow in a payments system. Here we'll examine the traditional consumer and merchant stakeholders, plus take a look at enterprises including businesses, billers, governments, and nonprofits.

In the next chapter, we'll continue our look at stakeholder perspectives—this time from the point of view of the providers of each payments system, including the banks, networks and clearing houses, processors, and payments services providers that play such a major role in payments systems.

The Consumer Perspective

With more than 305 million people now residing in the United States, the U.S. has the world's third-largest population—yet it represents only about 4.5% of the world's total population. The Census Bureau projects a U.S. population of 439 million by the year 2050. China (19.7%) and India (17.2%) are each several times larger, with Indonesia, the fourth largest (3.4%), just behind the U.S.

The U.S. is organized into more than 117 million households, about 87 million of which have traditional bank accounts. About 9 million households, or 17 million adults, make up a group often called "the unbanked," whose demographics are depicted in Table 8.1. Another 21 million households (43 million adults) are "underbanked," according to the FDIC.

	Unbanked	Underbanked
Adults	17,000,000	
Households	43,000,000	
Have open loop prepaid card	12.00%	16.00%
Receive income on payroll card	3.10%	4.20%

Table 8-1.
Unbanked and
Underbanked Consumers
Source: FDIC

Using FDIC definitions, "unbanked" refers to people who rarely, if ever, have held a checking, savings, or "other type of transaction or check-cashing account at an insured depository institution in the conventional finance system," while the "underbanked" have held bank or credit union accounts, but also rely on alternative payments and financial services, including check cashing services, payday loans, and the purchase of money orders.

Shifting Consumer Payments Behavior

Across the multiple domains of payments touched by individuals, consumer behavior continues to shift and change. Multiple studies have shown the shift to all forms of electronic payments and, in particular, the dramatic growth in debit card transaction volume—most commonly understood as replacing cash and checks. Figure 8-1 shows, over an eight year span, this radical shift in consumer payments behavior:

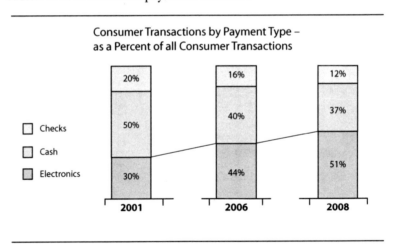

Figure 8-1.
Consumer Use of
Payments Systems
Source: Glenbrook

For example, at the point of sale for traditional purchases from local merchants, consumers increasingly prefer to pay with debit cards—shifting rapidly from cash and checks in particular. For everyday purchases, consumers also prefer debit cards over credit cards—although certain segments particularly conscious of credit card rewards continue to be loyal to those cards.

In eCommerce, historically the sole province of credit and debit cards, consumers are increasingly taking advantage of alternative payment options. Behavior shifts here seem to be driven primarily by consumer concerns about the safety of online shopping in some segments of the population; others aren't concerned, feeling adequately protected by their payment card zero-liability guarantees.

For recurring bill payments, consumers are shifting away from writing checks to either bill payment services (typically provided by banks as an adjunct to the checking account) or paying at the biller's website using a debit or credit card.

A few consumers are taking advantage of new services that allow person-to-person payments to, for example, settle a lunch tab or send money to children away at college. This is an area of particular focus for several mobile payments providers.

For receiving wages, most consumers instruct their employers to send payroll funds via ACH ("direct deposit") directly into a checking account. For certain segments of underbanked consumers, payroll cards provide another option—allowing them to avoid the fees associated with retail check cashing services.

Over time, the cumulative effects of these changes in consumer behavior will result in checks being a much smaller component of consumer payments, cash usage similarly declining, and card payments (especially debit cards but also credit cards) increasing in importance. Alternative payments will also continue to grow, but will remain relatively minor in terms of overall consumer payments behavior.

Factors Affecting Consumer Payments Behavior

Many factors play into the decision made by a consumer each time he or she needs to exchange value with another party—including practical considerations such as cost, convenience, familiarity, and frequency of use; earning rewards; taking advantage of credit extension; and timing of the payment. Other factors also play a role, including privacy/security sensitivities, perception of status, and influences from respected others.

Of all of these factors, rewards-based loyalty programs have had perhaps the greatest impact on credit card use over the last ten years. Reduced acceptance of checks by merchants has similarly helped accelerate consumer use of debit cards.

Gen Y	Gen X	Boomers	Seniors
Born 1975–2005	**1964–1974**	**1946–1964**	**Before 1946**
Debit card generation	Prefer debit over credit	Strong credit card orientation	Checks/cash orientation
Most likely to bank online	Strong use of all online services	Peak earning and spending power	Not sure about this ATM thing
Most likely to research and buy products online	Expect total transparency of products and services	Have the most credit cards, home equity loans, etc.	Credit card for emergencies
Living the mobile lifestyle		Prefer branch for major transactions	Branch banking for almost all transactions
			Phones are for talking

As illustrated in Table 8-2, demographics—particularly age-related factors—have been shown to influence consumer payment behavior. For example, younger individuals living a mobile lifestyle tend to be heavy users of debit cards, dislike checks, and bank and shop online. Baby boomers, at their peak in terms of earning and spending power, tend to be more rewards-oriented; many pay off their charges every month. Seniors tend to be the last bastion of checks, may still lack confidence in ATMs, and darken the bank branch doorways regularly!

"Carefree"	**"Careful"**
Only one of many possible sets of profiles!	
Don't keep track of balances	Keep track of account balances, limits, and expenditures
Pay bills when due—or later	Pay bills on schedule
May overdraw accounts or exceed limits	Don't overdraw
Pursue rewards only for the goodies	Pursue rewards even if not redeemed
Less security conscious	May be more security conscious
High convenience orientation	High financial rewards orientation

Table 8-3.
Consumer Payments
Behavior—Psychographics

Perhaps more telling than demographics, however, are the psychographic effects associated with consumer decisions about payments, as illustrated in Table 8.3. We all have various emotional relationships to money, and our decisions aren't always rational as a result. For example, some individuals, more carefree by nature, are much less worried about security than others who tend to be ultra-careful in their choices. Others are very cost-sensitive—even irrespective of their actual economic status. These psychographic effects result in it being difficult to project consumer choices based on just demographics.

Glenbrook's Theory on Consumer Adoption of New Payments Mechanisms

At Glenbrook, we've developed a simple theory about what really matters in shaping consumer behavior around new ways to pay: big increases in convenience and/or big perceived financial gains. Almost nothing else seems to matter.

Convenience helps instill confidence and inspires frequent usage. Anything that gets in the way of convenience—call it "friction"—is likely to dramatically reduce potential consumer acceptance.

Financial gains have to be significant to matter to consumers—significant enough to overcome existing habits and preferences about ways to pay. Rich rewards programs have demonstrated their ability to significantly influence consumer loyalty to a particular payment card, for example.

> ### The Lure of Convenience
>
> Although convenience is probably the largest single driver of new consumer payments success, it can also be an elusive goal. Any number of unsuccessful payments start-ups have been predicated on consumer convenience—only to founder when the actual convenience delivered fell short of the founders' vision. Early stored-value cards (with the value stored on a chip on the card) are a good example of this paradox. It seemed convenient at first—no cash!—but problems associated with not knowing the balance on the card, and running out of money at inopportune times, sank the consumer proposition.

One topic continues to confound payments providers. Consumers often say they care about security, and want more secure payment solutions - but often fail to adopt them when offered the option! At the end of the day, we must not forget that the actual making of a payment is not the consumer's real focus. Rather, consumers want to own the products they're purchasing, or experience the service, or pay off a liability incurred to another. That's where the rewards are—not in the payment mechanism itself!

Consumer Payments Markets We're Watching

As keen observers of the payments scene, we're particularly watching consumer adoption of new payments products and services for person-to-person payments—both for domestic transactions and for international remittances. The mobile handset—with its on-the-go interactivity with the consumer—seems the ideal way to initiate such payments. Time will tell just how important these payments are to consumers beyond the current niche segments now participating.

With such a significant segment of the U.S. population in the unbanked and underbanked categories, we're watching all the activity in the prepaid card space as various providers try to meet the needs of those segments for card-based payments. As card acceptance has become nearly ubiquitous (and cash, frankly, less so), these consumers seem to like the notion of a "bank on a card"—namely, a prepaid card. In the last five years, these open loop prepaid cards have been widely available, as distribution through supermarkets and other outlets has grown significantly. Reload of cash onto the cards is also widely available—further enhancing their utility.

Similarly, teens—traditionally unequipped to pay with payment cards—represent another opportunity for prepaid card providers.

Summary—Consumer Perspective

To summarize, consumer payments behavior is complex and influenced by many factors. We believe that convenience and financial incentives are the most powerful drivers affecting adoption of new ways to pay. Demographic factors, while not insignificant in importance, tend to be outweighed by consumer psychographic factors. Understanding and appealing to those factors are important keys to successful consumer payments behavior change.

The Merchant Perspective

According to the 2007 U.S. economic census, there are about 5 million retail establishments in the U.S. market. About 3 million of these are "non-employer" (also known as "mom and pop") establishments. All of these, by definition, accept one or more forms of payment. From a card industry perspective, there are approximately 15 million electronic point-of-sale terminals which enable the acceptance of payment cards at these merchant locations.

> ### Who's a Merchant?
>
> This term comes from the card industry, which refers to all card-accepting sellers as "merchants." Many of these enterprises don't think of themselves as merchants; rather, they're "retailers," "airlines," or "phone companies." In this book, we use the term to describe businesses that sell to consumers. We treat billers and enterprises serving mostly other businesses as separate classes of payments systems users.

Perhaps somewhat surprisingly, there's a high degree of concentration among the millions of merchants in the U.S. As it turns out, only some 350 major merchants are responsible for about half of all payment card transactions. Similarly, in the eCommerce world, the top 100 eRetailers account for over half the spending in their segment.

Naturally, major merchants have more power—and options—in dealing with payments choices than do smaller "mom and pop" merchants. Indeed, the largest merchants can afford dedicated staff who deal with payments acceptance decisions, infrastructure, costs, etc.

Merchants Just Want to Get Paid

> ### What Really Matters
>
> An important, but often overlooked, lesson in new payments adoption: At Glenbrook, we've seen a number of new product initiatives with the value proposition of reducing merchant payments costs fail or flounder. Meanwhile, other new products, with a "drive new merchant revenue" value proposition, have succeeded.

At the end of the day, what matters most to merchants is simply getting paid. After this, merchants are looking for payments solutions that will significantly increase sales. Solutions that focus on reducing costs, while not unimportant to merchants, are much less important than those that help drive higher revenues.

The introduction of the credit card offers an early example of the importance of driving higher sales. By simplifying the extension of credit to consumers, merchants who began accepting credit cards experienced higher sales, higher average tickets, and improved customer loyalty and satisfaction. Of course, there were costs involved—the "merchant discount"—but merchants were more than willing to pay in exchange for the increase in sales. After all, merchants take no credit risk on that increase; risk is handed off to the card issuer.

Get Paid	Sell More	Lower Costs
Payments can play a role—direct or indirect—in all of these strategies.		
Accept forms of payments that customers want to use Keep/make a sale when customers are undecided or wavering	Find new customers Increase loyalty of existing customers Increase customer spending power Increase speed of checkout process	Lower external costs of payments acceptance: fees, float, processing, risk management Lower internal cost of transaction handling: checkout process, systems integration, training Decrease incidents of fraud and theft

Table 8-4.
Merchant Payments
Motivations

Of course, costs do matter to merchants when they directly affect merchant profitability—and such costs do get attention where the staff exists to deal with them. Reducing operational costs, minimizing the costs of exception handling, and negotiating lower merchant discounts are all part of the equation for major merchants seeking to reduce the cost of payments acceptance. Similarly, eliminating check acceptance and shifting consumers to debit cards lets merchants reduce credit risk, fraud risk, and associated costs.

Payments Strategies to Drive Sales and Loyalty

Over the years, merchants have embraced several extensions to basic payment card acceptance—including issuing and accepting private label cards, participating in co-branded rewards-based card programs with credit card issuers, and selling and accepting prepaid gift cards. For most merchants, these tools help derive incremental sales revenues from the broadest possible set of consumers.

The Importance of Merchant Segmentation

The importance of the cost of payments can vary significantly by merchant segment. For example, virtual goods merchants selling digital content online are much less sensitive to the cost of payments, simply because their cost of goods sold is effectively zero. For others selling hard goods at low margins, the cost of payments can become critically important. Again, segmentation is important—one size doesn't fit all when it comes to merchants' payments acceptance needs.

eCommerce Merchants

In the last decade, the ecommerce merchant has captured the attention of the payments industry—certainly disproportionate to the value of eCommerce when compared to physical-world commerce. This reflects a fascination with the development and potential of online commerce, but also the unique payments challenges of the eCommerce merchant.

From the early days of online retailing, virtually all eCommerce payments were made by card (credit or signature debit). Yet the cards didn't work as well for the eCommerce merchant as for the physical-world merchant.

Looking Back: eCommerce in History

Long before Amazon.com opened its virtual doors, U.S. merchants were selling to customers in what became known as "card-not-present," or CNP, environments. These were most typically catalog sales made via mail or telephone order, and the segment became known as MOTO in the payments industry. MOTO merchants received money both by check and by card. The card industry considered MOTO a fraud-prone segment, as the merchant could not physically see the card being presented. Because of this, MOTO transactions were not fraud-guaranteed: if a consumer called his or her issuing bank and said "it wasn't me who ordered that," the issuing bank could credit the consumer's account and charge back the transaction to the acquiring bank, which would charge it back to the MOTO merchant's account.

When eCommerce began, the card industry simply extended this practice to online merchants. An eCommerce merchant must therefore manage card acceptance to avoid such fraud or to reduce it to an acceptable level. This is similar to what a physical world merchant does in accepting checks, with their risk of being bounced for insufficient funds or returned as fraudulent.

Merchant Frustrations with Payment Card Costs

Despite the benefits they receive from payment card acceptance, merchants have recently become increasingly vocal about the associated costs. Much of this frustration is the result of higher merchant discount fees charged on a new generation of rewards-based credit cards first introduced in the mid-2000's. At the time, Visa and MasterCard feared that issuing bank partners would find the interchange-like revenue share from American Express cards more lucrative than the Visa or MasterCard interchange. In response, they issued new card types with a wide range of consumer benefits, rewards, and features—and higher interchange for issuing banks. The funding source? Higher merchant discount fees.

Merchants have responded by lobbying regulators and legislators to enact new rules that would help lower fees. One major retailer is attempting to collect a million consumer signatures, to be forwarded to Congress as part of a lobbying effort.

Trends Affecting Merchant Payments Acceptance

Several other industry changes are underway, including the introduction of contactless cards—which can help penetrate previously unserved and cash-dominant merchant segments. Whether contactless achieves widespread merchant adoption (and card issuance) has yet to be seen; the incremental benefits over traditional magnetic stripe cards may not be great enough to make a positive business case for many merchants.

At the physical point of sale, merchants are replacing old dial-up connections with broadband—enabling faster transactions for consumers. Indeed, broadband is needed to fulfill the contactless value proposition for the consumer.

Some merchants, particularly those who serve as everyday purchase locations, are participating in merchant-funded reward programs as they attempt to influence consumer loyalty. Though these merchants pay a higher effective merchant discount when a participating card is used, they benefit from greater customer loyalty—and thus increased sales.

In another effort to lower acceptance costs, some merchants are embracing ACH-based payments. By displacing card transactions to ACH, merchants may be able to lower costs—as long as they can do so without taking on credit risk.

For several years, some merchants have been capturing check data at checkout and putting such payments through as ACH transactions, or imaging checks and depositing them electronically to their banks. These approaches offer significantly lower costs—in transaction processing and, more importantly, in the ability to represent a "bounced" check in a timely fashion.

In the online world, several companies are introducing push ACH payments. In these systems, the consumer must have good funds and authenticate to his or her bank before a payment can be initiated. While merchants benefit from lower costs, no credit or fraud risk, etc., some may have concerns about the "friction" involved in having consumers go down this path to make a payment.

Merchant Payments Environment

Because accepting a payment is only part of what a merchant actually does, any payments function requires some varying level of integration into the merchant's overall business environment and systems. This is another area in which segmentation is hugely important—and where endless complexity seems to reign as more and more industry-specific vendors incorporate payments functionality into their platforms.

In the last few years, the requirements placed on merchants to ensure compliance with the Payment Card Industry-Data Security Standard (PCI-DSS) have had a significant impact on merchant systems, back-office processes, etc. Major merchants that have suffered breaches in which payment card data has been exposed have been hit with significant financial penalties as a result. Priority number one on many a major merchant's to-do list: ensuring PCI-DSS compliance and successfully completing an independent assessment by a third-party assessor.

At the point of sale, merchants are dealing with acceptance requirements for new types of payments (contactless, mobile, etc.), along with their PCI-DSS effects.

Summary—Merchant Perspective

Merchant payments acceptance practices reflect a mix of what is required by customers to effect sales and what helps a merchant increase sales and reduce costs. Because merchants can be highly vocal on the subject of payments costs, it can be tempting to overlook the critical role of payments methods in increasing sales. But even a quick look at the most successful payments innovations of the last 25 years show that their ability to increase sales has been the primary motivation in merchant adoption: credit cards (increased purchasing power); gift cards (dedicated sales); and debit cards (increased convenience and speedier checkout).

> ### The Costs of PCI Compliance
>
> The card industry is still grappling with the magnitude of the card data security problem—and the costs of fixing it, or at least containing its damage. Perhaps most daunting is the necessity of a high level of continued investment ("security is a journey, not a destination"); recent fraudster attacks have demonstrated that even PCI compliance is not enough for full protection. As a result, many merchants are considering process outsourcing for payments—PaaS, or payments as a service.

The Biller Perspective

Billers, which include utility companies, mortgage servicers, insurance companies, telecommunications and cable TV providers, and others, are just another merchant segment. Altogether, over 100,000 billers handle about 22 billion payments per year in the U.S., in a complex acceptance environment that, again, varies by segment.

Billers need to support a broad range of consumer bill payment options, as shown in Table 8-5.

How	Where	What (Payments Systems)
In Person	Biller's office	Cash or check
	Agent's office or store	Cash, check, card
	Agent's kiosk	Some card only; others cash or card
Online	Online banking bill pay	Usually direct account debit, some support of cards
	Biller direct site	ACH eCheck or (some billers) cards
	Third party bill pay site	ACH eCheck or (some billers) cards
Standing Instructions	Given to biller online or through mail or phone	ACH preauthorized debit or card on file
By Phone	Bank IVR service	Usually direct account debit, some support of cards
	Biller IVR service	ACH eCheck or (some billers) cards
	Third party IVR service	ACH eCheck or (some billers) cards

Table 8-5.
Bill Payment Options

The most common consumer bill pay practice is still mailing in a check. Increasingly, however, consumers find it more convenient to pay bills on-line—at either a bank's bill payment site or the biller's own website. Some billers accept payments via phone/IVR; others, especially in the wireless and cable TV segments, take payments at walk-in storefront locations.

We see consumers paying bills at home, at the biller's storefront, at agent storefront locations, and online as mentioned above.

When bills get paid also varies. Some consumers give some billers a standing instruction to deduct funds from their checking accounts or charge a particular payment card each month. Others wait until the last minute to pay—rushing to the biller's "direct" website to complete the payment and receive same-day credit for it. More traditionally, some consumers schedule mailing bill payments based on due dates. Others use banks or a third-party provider such as Western Union to make same-day rush payments, avoiding service interruption or significant late payment fees.

The tender type also varies, based on the other dimensions of bill payment. For example, use of cash makes sense only in a face-to-face payment scenario. Some billers, particularly those serving many cash-centric consumers, support walk-in bill payments primarily to facilitate taking cash. A biller wishing to take payment cards needs a traditional merchant agreement with a payment card acquirer, and with a bank for eCheck or ACH debit payments.

> ### *Checks: Not Dead Yet*
>
> A dizzying number of consumer bill payment surveys regularly appear. All confirm the same basic message: the use of checks is going down, and consumers are preferring various forms of electronic payments to checks. It is also clear, however, that no one form of electronic payment is going to "win": billers will have to continue to accept multiple types of electronic and paper payments for the indefinite future.

Not surprisingly, billers tend to use common practices to support the various channels and payment methods. Billers receiving large quantities of checks, for example, often use an outsourced "lockbox" to pick up the incoming mail, scan it, and receive post-process details for posting to their accounts receivable systems. The card networks have been encouraging biller-direct websites—which commonly support payment cards as their preferred payment method. Alternatively, they may support eCheck (ACH) payments, although more complexity and increased credit risk makes this option less attractive for some billers.

Today, biller direct is winning the online bill payment battle—having moved ahead of bank bill payment services in the last few years.

Billers Perspectives on Payments

As with merchants generally, it's important to understand that payments acceptance cost is only one consideration in terms of the biller's choice of supported payment methods. Some biller segments want to attract consumers to their websites to cross-market new products and features. Others (such as mortgage servicers), for which marketing additional products makes little or no sense, are unlikely to want to spend money on a robust biller-direct website. For many billers, eliminating the operational costs of mailing paper statements is a big financial deal—and PTO (paper turn off) is their holy grail. Others may decide that they want to encourage late payments, thereby driving fee income above and beyond the actual bill amount owed.

The range of biller motivations is described in Table 8-6.

Segment	Objective	Common Strategies
All billers	Reduce statement expense	Encourage customers to come to biller's website (perhaps by accepting online credit and debit card payments)
Credit card issuers, cable, telephone billers	Cross-sell (especially credit card, telephone, cable, and online services billers)	
Utilities	Encourage customer self-service	
All billers	Lower payments acceptance costs	Use more ACH; avoid card acceptance Charge "convenience fees" for cards
Education, local tax	Comply with card network regulations	Limit "convenience fees" to online channel
Utilities	Comply with industry regulators	Use third parties to accept card payments: convenience fees go direct to third party
Mortgage processors, telephone billers, cable	Collect late payment fee revenue	Make late payments by phone or online convenient for customers; accept card payments

Table 8-6. Biller Payments Motivations

Reducing payments acceptance costs is important—but often secondary to the primary aspects of payments acceptance just discussed.

The trends we're watching with respect to billers include how credit card issuers are working to educate cardholders about online bill payment and its benefits. Some banks are beginning to worry about the costs of providing online bill payment services—especially in the face of accelerated consumer adoption of biller-direct payments. Kiosk-based bill payment (enabling cash intake, for example, at unattended locations) is increasingly important for the unbanked segment. And mobile phone technology seems potentially useful for notifying consumers of pending bills—not to mention as a way for the consumer to actually initiate bill payment.

Summary—Biller Perspective

Each biller's perspective on payments is colored not only by considerations of cost and efficiency, but also by its other business objectives. For many biller segments, getting close to the customer is important: for cross-sales opportunities, for customer self-service, or to increase the chance of delivering statements electronically. Such billers may want to draw customers to their websites for these reasons, offering incentives (or accepting a higher cost of payments) to achieve that goal.

The Enterprise Perspective

There are more than 27 million enterprises in the United States—including businesses, nonprofit organizations, educational institutions, and local governments and agencies. The U.S. Census Bureau breaks down businesses by the number of employees; not surprisingly, these numbers are represented by a steep pyramid, with the vast majority of enterprises having 20 or fewer employees.

The merchants and billers discussed above are included in these enterprise numbers. The discussion in this section concerns enterprises other than those defined as merchants or billers.

Enterprise Payments Requirements

Even the smallest businesses have payments requirements similar to those of the largest companies. For example, businesses must control cash flow through the scheduling of payments. The ability to forecast cash inflows and outflows is fundamental to ensure the ongoing solvency and viability of an enterprise. Security and fraud risk protections are important—increasingly so as the size of the enterprise's bank accounts grow.

On the cost side, businesses want to maximize the efficiency of their accounts receivables and accounts payables functions. They seek to minimize the fees they pay to banks and third parties for services, and to ensure accelerated access to good funds received.

> **Shifting Risks**
>
> For enterprises, changes in payments systems used—at their own initiative or that of their *counterparties*—can bring risk management challenges. Controls which work to manage check fraud, for example, may not apply to ACH or card transactions—which demand their own risk management processes. Also, some provisions of ACH and card network rules, and federal regulations, provide protections for consumers but do not afford equivalent protections for enterprises.

Both large and small companies need to integrate payments data into the systems that run their companies. For small businesses, this tends to mean PC-based (or, increasingly, online) accounting packages. A larger enterprise will use one or more ERP (enterprise resource planning) systems to run its business.

Choosing Payments Providers

Decisions about what payments types to use—and which providers to choose—vary considerably by size of company.

- A very small enterprise will usually manage payments very much like a consumer does, often with the same bank used by the owner of the business.

- A medium-sized enterprise, particularly one that is growing, is often dependent on a bank or banks for the extension of credit. Many enterprises award basic payments business (a checking account, and check or electronic collections or disbursements) to their credit bank. A medium-sized enterprise will, as it grows, add payments providers other than the primary bank—another bank to support a regional requirement, for example, or a non-bank card acquirer or payroll processor.

- A large enterprise will treat the acquisition and management of payments services just as it does any other important business process required by the firm. A decision to select a new payments provider will lead to the use of RFPs and a competitive bidding process. Very large enterprises have sophisticated cash management processes and complex relationships with several large banks, who compete for the high-volume, lucrative payments streams of the enterprise.

Within the enterprise, checks remain the dominant form of payment, with more than 70% of large enterprise payments made via check. We've watched and waited for years for this percentage to accelerate its decline—but it stubbornly hangs in there. The check percentage for smaller enterprises is even higher; the check remains the universally convenient way to pay.

There is considerable complexity in managing the enterprise payments function in this largely paper-based payments environment. In particular, it is critically important to ensure that payments received are properly accounted for by matching them to appropriate remittance data. Similarly, to help prevent fraud, enterprises must ensure that all checks sent are securely linked to positive pay accounts. Finally, all enterprises must constantly handle exceptions—especially larger enterprises where customers may take arbitrary (so-called "self-awarded") discounts on the amount of an invoice paid, etc.

Summary—Enterprise Perspective

Most enterprises have common payments management goals: ensuring control and timing of payments, efficiency of operations, and avoidance of risk. As companies grow, the need to interact with more and more counterparties makes payments management increasingly complex.

Summary: Payments Systems Users

Payments systems users want convenience, security, and reliability in payments systems. But both consumers and merchants have complex motivations, particularly around financial incentives—both positive and negative—in using payments systems.

Perspectives on Payments Systems Providers

Introduction

This chapter continues a two-part look at the stakeholders that participate in any payments system. In the prior chapter, we explored the users of a payments system—in particular, the senders and receivers of the funds that flow in a payments system.

In this chapter, we look at providers of services in a payments system: banks, networks and clearing houses, and processors (which play a major behind-the-scenes role in payments systems).

The Bank Perspective

Historically, banks have owned and controlled the major payments systems in the United States. Consumers and enterprises have used the payments systems through their roles as bank customers. Banks, too, have been the primary direct economic beneficiaries of the payments system.

However, banks' status in this area is now changing, with some payments systems no longer owned by banks, and nonbank players emerging in significant roles.

> **Terminology Reminder** The term "bank" in this section is used to include banks, thrifts, savings banks, and credit unions.

Bank Segmentation

As shown in Table 9.1, banks in the U.S. can be loosely segmented based upon market focus (global, national, regional, or local). The large global banks serve consumer and enterprise clients in many, if not most, countries around the world. National banks have large branch footprints and serve customers across the U.S. Regional banks focus on customers in specific geographic regions. Thousands of much smaller community banks and credit unions serve local clientele.

Global Focus Institutions	National Focus Institutions	Regional Focus Institutions
Citibank	Bank of America	U.S. Bank
Barclay's	JPMorgan Chase	SunTrust
HSBC	Wells Fargo	PNC Bank
Deutsche Bank		Dozens of other large regionals and hundreds of smaller regionals
ABN AMRO		
Many others		
Local Focus Institutions	**Special Purpose Institutions**	
8,000 + community banks	The Federal Reserve Banks	
7,800 + credit unions	Industrial loan corporations (ILCs)	
	"Banker's banks"	
	Securities processing banks (BNY Mellon, State Street)	
	Credit card "monolines"	

Table 9-1.
Banks in the United States

Not all depository institutions or all categories are listed.

There are also a number of special-purpose banks including the Federal Reserve Banks themselves, industrial loan companies (such as Target), credit card "monolines" (such as American Express and Discover), the former investment banks (Goldman Sachs, Morgan Stanley, etc.), securities-focused banks (State Street, BNY Mellon and others).

Over the last few years, the banking industry has continued to consolidate, with the total number of financial institutions declining. Perhaps paradoxically, however, the number of bank branch locations in the U.S. has continued to grow—a trend partially fueled by the practice of co-locating branches in retail stores, supermarkets, etc.

In terms of concentration based upon share of total deposits, it's still a relatively unconcentrated business—the top three U.S. banks represent only about 26.5% of deposits (i.e., funds sitting in consumer and business checking accounts in banks, thrifts, and credit unions). When viewed in terms of debit card purchase volume, the top three account for about 35% of total purchase volume.

> ### Processors Support a Broad Market
>
> Compared to other countries, the U.S. is a very unconcentrated banking market. There are many reasons for this, going back to the days when regulation prevented interstate banking. Today, the payments processors are one of the factors supporting an unconcentrated structure. The large processors, offering not just payments but lending, general ledger, and bank management systems, enable a single-branch or small regional bank to operate very much as if it were a division of a larger bank. Through the processors, the bank can clear checks, ACHs, and debit card and ATM card transactions very much as a large bank might use an in-house regional processing center.

Understanding Banks

Banks are Regulated

In the U.S., to start a bank, you need a charter from an issuing agency—a state or federal chartering authority. The chartering authority examines the business plan, management competency, and capital adequacy of the proposed bank. The charter, when issued, defines the capabilities of the bank. The key activity is deposit taking: a non-bank can lend money or handle payments, but only a chartered institution can accept consumer deposits into a transaction account. Banks are audited and examined on an ongoing basis, often by multiple regulatory agencies; these agencies have the power to revoke a bank's charter, among other actions, if dissatisfied with its performance. The primary federal regulatory bodies in the United States are the Federal Reserve Bank, the FDIC (Federal Deposit Insurance Corporation), the OCC (Office of the Comptroller of the Currency), and the Office of Thrift Administration. State-chartered banks are regulated by state banking authorities.

How Banks Make Money

Banks make money by lending money, by holding money (in deposit accounts or investment accounts), and by moving money—moving money means payments. Although all three activities are profitable for banks, the relative profits are highest for lending, and lending activities tend to dominate a bank's management agenda. Deposit taking is profitable on its own, but is particularly valued as a source of funds for the more profitable lending business.

> ### A History of Interoperability
>
> It is interesting to contrast banking with an industry such as health care in the United States. Today, hospitals and doctors are trying to figure out how to exchange electronic medical records, but the institutions do not have the history of interoperability that financial institutions (or, for another example, telecommunications firms) do, so they face a steeper learning curve.

Historically, payments were seen not as a line of business, but rather as an operational support function that enabled lending and deposit taking. The "productization" of the payments business has evolved within banks in fits and starts. The credit card issuing business quickly grew into a separate P&L item within most banks—a clear line of business. Retail checking accounts are considered a line of business in most banks; these encompass account deposits and the payments activities (checks, ATMs, debit cards, ACHs) that consumers run through accounts. Again historically, commercial payments accounts were offered as a free service to corporations with substantial balances at the bank. When interest rates spiked in the late 1970s and corporations began to pull out their bank balances for investment, this "service" evolved into today's cash management business line; banks responded by pricing payments services.

Many large and regional banks have profitable correspondent banking businesses, which provide payments services to smaller banks.

Banks are Interoperable

From the early days of check clearing houses, banks have understood the need to interoperate. Banks are sophisticated network members, and understand how consortia should be formed and managed.

Banks are Technology Savvy

Banks were early and enthusiastic adopters of technology. Many of the routine tasks of banking, including payments processing, were well suited to automation, and the grind of the nightly "batch run," when check payments and deposits were posted to DDA accounts, became the mainstay of bank IT managers and their mainframe suppliers. In the 1980s, banks began large-scale implementation of ATMs and, shortly thereafter, the ATM networks that grew to enable debit cards at the point of sale.

Banks were also early adopters of customer-facing online applications. Early online banking applications predated the Internet by at least a decade. Again, the simplicity of tasks involved ("Check my balance"; "Pay the phone company $50") was well suited to automation; perhaps more significantly, the frequency of interaction drove bankers' interest in online banking.

Today, many large banks have core legacy systems for running DDAs and lending platforms that have remained largely untouched for, in some cases, decades. Banks have managed changing product, feature, and compliance requirements by wrapping ever more sophisticated layers of middleware around these core platforms.

Large banks have also become extremely adept managers of technology integration following bank mergers. Wall Street measures the efficiency of bank integration closely.

In recent years, banks have increased investment in technology to meet compliance requirements (only some of which are payments-related).

> #### The Amazing ATM
>
> It's hard to imagine, from the standpoint of the present, just how innovative and frankly amazing the ATM was. Customers who once spent their lunch hours waiting in line to deposit a paycheck and get grocery money could now take care of business on their way home from work—or after church on Sunday.
>
> Many bankers thought, in the early days of ATMs, that branches would eventually go away. In fact, over time, banks have learned that each new customer channel (ATMs, customer call centers, online banking, mobile banking) simply adds a new layer, without supplanting the earlier channels!

Risk Managers

Banks must, of course, be risk managers: risk management is at the heart of the lending business and is an essential component of both deposit and payments businesses. Beyond simply understanding risk and how to manage it, banks grasp the relationship between risk and profit: their most profitable businesses (most definitely including credit card issuance) demand proactive assumption of risk. Bank strategies with respect to risk management vary considerably. One credit card issuer, for example, might choose to issue cards to many consumers with relatively low credit scores, and manage performance on these accounts closely; another might choose to issue fewer cards to better customers, and give each customer a large line and more leeway.

Relationships and Products

Banks are fundamentally relationship companies: most share the strategy of trying to cross-sell multiple products to their customers. This is true for both large and small banks, and for both consumer and commercial businesses within a bank. Many large banks measure senior managers on cross-selling success.

Banks often prioritize investments in relationship capabilities (for example, cross-bank information portals) over investments in new or enhanced product features. In fact, banks do not have a good track record on new product development. If, for example, you were to examine a list of a bank's major products today and fifty years ago, you would find very little difference in what is offered to customers—but a great deal of difference in how it is offered. Yesterday's checking account looks a lot like today's—but today's checking account has a debit card and ATM, online, and mobile access.

Banks and Their Customers

Banks have a uniquely challenging relationship with their customers. Customers tend to trust their banks, but sadly, often don't like them. Consumers, in particular, have contradictory feelings about banks' stewardship of their money. They value the safety and convenience of the bank, but many are outraged at the idea that a bank might charge them for these services. It's not uncommon to hear, "It's my money—they're making money on me somehow."

Banks and Payments

Banks like the payments business for many reasons. Payments are often the reason a customer (consumer or commercial) opens an account with the bank, and are often seen as "sticky"—heavy payments users are less likely to move business to another bank. The payments business is more stable, and less risky, than the bank's lending businesses, and the revenue from the payments business (e.g., interchange or float) is often invisible to customers, and therefore less likely to trigger problems with customer attitudes toward pricing.

> **The Paradox of Free Checking**
>
> This attitude on the part of consumers led retail bankers to develop the concept of "free checking." Free checking is free, of course, only if your balances are high enough. Retail bankers also supplement their income through bounced check and overdraft fees, and through debit card interchange—which is invisible to the consumer.
>
> Consumer attitudes toward the pricing of payments services make life complicated—to put it mildly—for both banks and nonbank competitors providing consumer payments services.

> **Payments—Big Businesses for Banks**
>
> In 2007, Bank of America released a study showing that 52% of its corporate revenues were associated with payments; of those, 43% were from credit card accounts, 30% from consumer demand deposit accounts, and 16% from corporate accounts. The bank further broke out payment revenue by type: net interest income (including interest and the value of balances in accounts) accounted for 57% of payments revenue, fees for 33%, and interchange for 10%.

Summary—Bank Perspective

The U.S. banking industry is unconcentrated, with thousands of banks needing to interoperate, particularly for payments systems. Banks value their payments businesses for the customers and revenue it brings, although they manage some payments activities as services rather than standalone products. Customer trust of banks is an asset for the payments business, but customer ambivalence about banks charging for services represents a challenge for banks.

The Network Perspective
What is a Network?

In this section, we discuss those companies or groups that provide one or more of the three key functions of an open loop payments system: rules, brand, and processing (in particular, intermediary switching and settlement). It should be noted that there is considerable overlap between the concepts of "network" and "processor": many networks do some processing, and many processors operate transaction switches and/or own networks. Closed loop payments system operators, in particular, can be seen as both networks and processors.

Most payments networks in the U.S. began life as nonprofit bank-owned consortia. Today, some remain so, while others are, or are owned by, public companies. Regardless of the ownership structure, most networks subscribe to a principle of equal treatment of members.

Network Economics and Challenges

Most networks charge for their services on a fixed-fee basis. As such, they have in common with processors the need to operate at scale to cover fixed costs, particularly of operating switching and settlement platforms. Some networks (notably Visa and MasterCard in the U.S.) also charge a very small *ad valorem* fee.

Networks tend to be volume-hungry: they actively seek new or underpenetrated markets, and compete with other payments networks for this volume.

Networks face a brand challenge: a recognizable and well-understood brand, with positive attributes associated with it, improves the networks' ability to grow volume—but may conflict with member banks' preferences that the bank brand dominate.

The Hand That Rules

Much of the drama in the payments industry is played out in network committee rooms during rules debates. A single rule, or clause in a rule, can radically reshape the economics of the business.

The biggest power of a network is its rule-making authority. In exercising this authority, the network needs to balance the loud voices of its largest users against the quieter voices of many small users. Historically, many payments systems rules were kept secret from the public, and made available only to participating members. (Famously, Visa and MasterCard used to require acquiring bank contracts to bind merchants to their rules—without letting the merchants see the rules! Today, both organizations make the rules available on their websites.)

The Processor Perspective

Who are the Processors?

The term "processor" is perhaps the least understood in the payments industry—in fact, there is no single definition for it. The term means different things within different payments systems and when used by different constituents to each system. For the purposes of this section, processors include:

- Companies that provide "on behalf of" transaction or account handling for banks, merchants, billers, or enterprises.

- Companies that provide private switching services for a group of banks, merchants, billers, or enterprises (but that are not included in the definition of "network" above).

- Companies that provide single- or narrow-function capabilities related to payments. This very broad category includes credit bureaus, bill pay processors, lockbox processors, security and authentication services, risk managers, collections services, and many others.

- Companies that provide hardware and/or software related to payments. This includes terminal manufacturers, card manufacturers, check stock printers, check sorters, ACH and wire transfer software processors, etc.

Processor Challenges and Economics

Transaction handling processing is almost always a fixed-fee business (charging transaction fees, periodic maintenance fees, etc.), although there are some situations in which a processor participates in a float benefit, for example, or holds funds in escrow for a period of time. Large-scale processors often describe their business as one in which the very largest clients provide the volume for scale economies, but demand prices so low as to be virtually break-even, while the smaller clients pay higher prices that essentially provide the profit for the business model—Figure 9-1 shows the breakdowns here. Processors, in search of volume, often supply the same, or similar, services to banks and bank customers; managing this channel conflict is one of the requirements of the business. (See Card Acquiring, Chapter 5, for a more detailed discussion on card acquiring processing.)

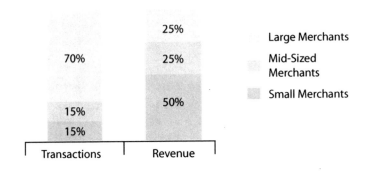

Figure 9-1.
Processor Economics
Source: Glenbrook

Software suppliers are seeing a major shift in their business mix. Many software companies have parallel offerings—software is either licensed to a bank or merchant (and often priced on a transaction basis) or hosted at the software company; hosting can be as a dedicated application for each customer or on a shared platform. Software suppliers compete with in-house IT teams at major banks; particularly in the card business, there has been a great deal of shift as credit card issuers have consolidated.

Payments Services Providers

A special category of non-bank payments providers serve end parties directly. Consumer-facing payments services providers include check cashing companies, bill payment companies, prepaid card issuers, and money transfer services (such as Western Union and MoneyGram). There are also consumer- and merchant-facing payments services providers, particularly in the eCommerce domain—PayPal, eBillme, Google Checkout, etc. Definitions here are slippery, of course: one could categorize closed loop card networks (such as American Express) and merchants offering private-label credit, debit, or prepaid cards as being "payments services providers", as well.

Payments services providers must invest in the brand and market channels necessary to reach their end parties directly. They may provide processing (transaction handling, account opening, customer service) themselves, or contract with other processors to provide it. If such providers are funding payment transactions from other payment accounts (for example, from credit cards, debit cards, or direct access to bank accounts), they typically make arrangements with one or more banks that are members of the necessary networks. Similarly, if they are handling outbound payments through established networks, they need to make arrangements for this. Many payments services providers handle cross-border payments; to do so, they may establish private networks of banks (which have correspondent relationships with each other) to process and clear transactions. Payments services providers may, over time, develop significant "on-us" volumes, and can process these transactions internally, without relying on external banks or networks.

The economic models of payments services providers are usually complex, and reflect a mix of direct revenues from end parties (merchant discount fees, for example, or consumer fees) and indirect revenue from float, foreign exchange fees, and, in certain situations, interchange fees shared with a bank partner. In addition to the routine expenses of managing their business, payments services providers usually assume some degree of risk in handling transactions, and must invest in the capability to manage acceptable levels.

Summary: Payments Systems Providers

Providers play many different roles in payments systems. Some roles are infrastructural—deep in the plumbing of the systems. These providers offer intermediary switching, processing, or supporting services, and are often invisible to the end parties to a transaction. Other providers are highly visible to both consumers and merchants. Many providers, including banks, processors, networks, and payments services providers, play roles that encompass both infrastructural and customer-facing elements. Providers in the payments industry face challenges in acquiring the scale necessary for cost-efficient processing. Higher margins often accrue more to those providers able to charge *ad valorem*, or a percentage of the dollar value of transactions processed, than to those charging flat fees for transaction processing.

Emerging Payments

Frameworks and Definitions

Emerging and alternative payments are the focus of a great deal of interest, experimentation, and investment in the U.S. payments industry. In this section, we introduce a few definitions and explore the major areas of activity.

What are emerging payments?

Glenbrook defines an emerging payment as a new product, from an existing or new player, that offers the payment user a new or significantly different method of initiating a payment.

Every payment transaction must be initiated, funded, and completed. The relative timing of these processes can vary by system and type of provider.

Figure 10-1.
A Simple Payments Value Chain

Figure 10-1 depicts a simple payments value chain. Most (though not all) emerging payments solutions concentrate on payment initiation, and use existing payments products and systems to manage the funding and completion (delivery of payment to recipient) parts of the value chain. Because of this, we generally don't consider such emerging products new payments systems. A contactless card transaction is an excellent example: the method by which the card payment is conducted is different, but the underlying way the transaction is funded (as either a debit card or credit card) and how the merchant account is settled are unchanged.

Another common theme in emerging payments is "doubling up". As shown in Figure 10-2, the payments service replaces a single payment transaction with two transactions. Bank-based online bill payment is a good example of this. Before online banking, a customer might have written a check to a utility company: a single transaction. In contrast, when a customer using online bill payment authorizes a transaction, the bank debits the customer's account and credits the bank's own account (the first transaction). The bank then initiates, most typically, an ACH credit transaction to pay the utility company; this transaction is likely to aggregate payments from multiple customers (the second transaction).

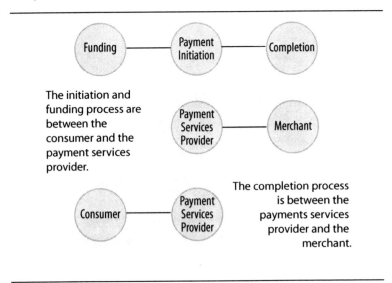

Figure 10-2.
Doubling Up Payments

Non-bank providers are aggressive entrants into the emerging payments space. Many seek to establish consumer and merchant brands, and to use existing bank payments systems (most typically ACH) to actually move the money.

Where the Action Is in Emerging Payments

Glenbrook tracks emerging payments developments by technology and domain. Here's what we're watching:

Enabling Technologies

A convergence of technological developments is enabling a proliferation of emerging payments products and companies. The key technologies we are watching include:

- The Internet and eCommerce

- The mobile Internet, mobile phone applications, and mobile commerce

- Web 2.0, and particularly the community-based conventions

- Social media

- Chips, both on cards and in phones (NFC, or near field communications)

- Cloud computing and "payments as a service"

- Neural networking and other risk-management capabilities

- Check imaging

Mobile is arguably the most significant technology for payments at this time. At Glenbrook, people often ask us, "What are mobile payments?" The answer, we believe, is *"Ask not what mobile payments are—ask how payments fit into a mobile world."* We are following new products and companies that are introducing payments effected by, enabled by, used by, and supported by mobile telephones. These products represent not a new domain, but rather capabilities emerging across the payments domains.

The Point of Sale Domain

- Contactless cards, mobile NFC (phone-based) pilots, and assorted alternatives to NFC, including some SMS payments, with offerings from Bling Nation, Blaze Mobile, Mocapay, mFoundry, and others.

- Open loop prepaid cards increasing in functionality.

- Mobile phone payments acceptance, for both traditional merchants and a newly defined class of "micro merchants," with offerings from VeriFone, Intuit, and Square, among others.

- ACH-based products, using either proprietary cards (private label ACH cards such as the Shell Saver card) or a card or other token from a payments service provider (e.g., the National Payment Card). The "decoupled debit" card introduced by Capital One falls into this category.

- Ongoing tests and pilots for unattended environments, including tollbooths (the Mobil SpeedPass is the grandfather here) and vending machines.

- The introduction of closed loop *contactless* cards in urban transit systems.

- An ongoing debate about the merits of moving to EMV chip technology at the U.S. point of sale.

The eCommerce Domain

- The online payments services providers: PayPal, Google, and Amazon.com.

- PayPal's X Platform and Amazon.com's Flexible Payment Service—platforms to enable developers to build payments applications into their services.

- Micropayment and digital content purchasing enablers, many of which use mobile platforms or a combination of online and mobile platforms; some of these use "bill to carrier" mobile payments models for transaction funding. Examples include BOKU, ZONG, Payfone, and Danal.

- Payment services that access a consumer's DDA account, either through ACH (Mazooma), PIN debit (Acculynk, Verient), or bank bill pay (eBillme, Moneta); also, warranty or verification services that help merchants initiate ACH payments on their own (First Data TeleCheck, FIS Global Certegy).

- Payments services that help eCommerce merchants selling subscription-based services with recurring payments requirements, including Vindicia and Aria Systems.

The Bill Payment Domain

- Mobile banking with embedded bill payment
- Mobile bill payment on a "biller direct" model
- Continued growth in the use of ACH eChecks at billers' Web and phone sites
- Connecting prepaid cards to bill payment, to support unbanked consumers
- Changes in online banking bill payment that allow consumers to use credit or debit cards to fund transactions

Person-to-Person Payments

- Mobile phone-initiated payments, domestic and cross-border, from both incumbents (Western Union, MoneyGram) and start-ups (Obopay, Blaze Mobile, mPayy, and many others)

- Card-to-card payments using the card networks to "push" money: Visa Money Transfer and MasterCard MoneySend

Business-to-Business Payments

- A second wave of B2B payments networks, including Bottomline's Paymode-X and the Visa/U.S. Bank joint venture Syncada

- New products focused on small business payments, including Intuit's PaymentNetwork

- Continued growth of both ACH and cards for supplier payments

- New efforts to solve the "supplier directory" problem in B2B payments

Income Payments

- Continued growth in payroll cards, and in the use of direct deposit to electronically deposit salary or benefits payments to other open loop prepaid cards

---

What it Takes to Succeed in Emerging Payments

We're often asked what it takes to succeed in emerging payments. Here are some of our answers:

Solve the Chicken-and-Egg Problem

A payments system needs to provide compelling benefits for both the payer and the payee of a transaction. In addition, it must have enough merchants on board (to use a consumer purchase example) to interest consumers, and enough consumers on board to interest merchants. See the problem?

Get the Economic Model Right

It isn't always obvious, in payments, who the paying customer is. Is it the payer or the payee? Both? Are the charges visible, or invisible, to one or both end parties? Is there an *ad valorem* (percentage of value) component? Most important, is the provider proactively assuming risk?

> **Risk and Return**
>
> Providers that proactively assume risk tend to make more money. That's fine, but the real problem is when a company assumes risk—and doesn't understand that it's doing so! Such companies don't last too long.

An often-overlooked part of the economic model is the cost of customer acquisition—something credit card industry veterans are very familiar with. "Viral marketing" is a great concept, but often not strong enough to support a new payment product's requirements.

Understand How to Operate in Scale

Payments systems that are successful tend to get very big—very fast. There is little tolerance, on the part of end parties, for systems that don't work right, with a very, very high degree of reliability. So providers need to be ready for large volumes and broad geographic coverage. This requires investment in technology and operations, of course, but also in such infrastructural components as risk management, rules writing and administration, and regulatory compliance.

Looking Ahead—What's Next for Payments

At Glenbrook, we love to see innovation in payments. We evaluate many new payments concepts and companies—often for our clients, and sometimes just for ourselves. We also forecast markets and make predictions about the success of individual innovations. Of course, sometimes we're right and sometimes we're wrong. We're pleased if we've called something correctly – and we think we're right more often than we're wrong. But we're humbled any time we miss new markets or ideas and, along with the rest of the industry, have to play catch-up. (An example of what we've missed? The emergence of a third-party distribution model in prepaid cards.) So we're always ready to believe that there is some new innovation—in technology, business models, or marketing—that we haven't seen or predicted.

If you have thoughts or ideas, let us know (ideas@glenbrook.com). You can follow what we're watching on our news site, www.paymentsnews.com, and hear what we're thinking about on www.paymentsviews.com. Let's keep up the innovation!

Index

CPSIA information can be obtained at www.ICGtesting.com
Printed in the USA
BVOW051234041211

277548BV00003B/49/P